Telling the Bible 2

A Lion Book
an imprint of
Lion Hudson plc
Mayfield House, 256 Banbury Road,
Oxford OX2 7DH, England
www.lionhudson.com
ISBN 0 7459 5188 0

First edition 2005
10 9 8 7 6 5 4 3 2 1 0

Acknowledgments
p. 139–40 'The Way We Were'. Lyrics by Marilyn and Alan
Bergman. Copyright © 1973. Produced by Columbia Records.
p. 140–41 'The Times They are a-Changing'. Words by Bob
Dylan. Copyright © 1963; renewed 1991 Special Rider Music.
p. 144 'I Still Haven't Found What I'm Looking For'. Words
by Bono. Copyright © 1983. Produced by Island Records.

Scripture quotations taken from the Holy Bible, New International
Version, copyright © 1973, 1978, 1984 International Bible Society.
Used by permission of Zondervan and Hodder & Stoughton Ltd.
All rights reserved. The 'NIV' and 'New International Version'
trademarks are registered in the United States Patent and
Trademark Office by International Bible Society. Use of either
trademark requires the permission of International Bible Society.
UK trademark number 1448790.

A catalogue record for this book is available
from the British Library

Typeset in 10.5/14 Aldine721 BT
Printed and bound in Great Britain
by Cox & Wyman Ltd, Reading

Telling the Bible 2

More Stories and Readings
for Sharing Aloud

Bob Hartman

LION

Contents

Introduction

A couple of years ago, at *Spring Harvest*, I was asked to read a passage from the Bible before the speaker got up to deliver his evening message. As I sat in my chalet, reading the text, the storyteller in me took over! I saw a line in the passage that made a good chorus – something simple and fun that everyone could repeat. So I reshaped the text with that in mind, and the crowd seemed to really enjoy it.

I was asked to do the same on the following few nights as well and, when I got home, I had a look at some of the other readings and short stories I had written over the years. Many of them were aimed at children or at all-age gatherings, but there were quite a few others that had a lot more to say to adults. So I thought, Why not put them together into some kind of collection? Why not drop in a few suggestions for telling them as well – to make them easier to use? Why not see if others could find some use for them – in worship or in teaching or in small groups or even for personal meditation? And that's where *Telling the Bible* came from.

As it happens, people did find those readings helpful, and they have used them in all the situations I hoped they would. And so, trusting that if fifty readings are good, then a hundred are even better, here is *Telling the Bible 2*!

I have taken the same basic approach as in the first book. The pieces are placed in the order of the Bible books, so they are easier to find. There are pieces that can be used in connection with the major Christian seasons and festivals. Most of the stories have been 'road-tested' (thanks again to the people at Bethesda Baptist Church!), so I'm reasonably confident that they 'work'. And that's why there are 'Telling Tips' for most stories, although some of them do lend themselves to simply being told without any kind of participation. And, finally, as with the first book, please feel free to adapt the stories to meet your needs.

As you will see, however, there are some differences between this book and the last one. For a start, the readings, on the whole, are shorter. This is mainly because I had the best feedback on the shorter pieces in *Telling the Bible*. I think there's a lot to be said for saying what you have to say in a punchy way, and I think this book reflects that. The book also reflects my own growing interest in the connections between storytelling and music. And so you will find several 'Songs in Search of a Tune' in this collection – some of which are stories and some of which you might simply like to present as poems. But, hey, if you come up with a good tune for any of them, do let me know! I have also included a few stories that depend on musical accompaniment, and a few others that tie in to the *Spring Harvest 2005* theme of singing the Lord's song in an increasingly secular, foreign land.

Finally, as I said in the first book, I find that there's nothing more interesting than crawling into a text, asking questions and then coming out the other side again, having discovered something brand new about what God has to say there – and also a new way of saying it! As you use this book, as you 'tell' the Bible, I hope that this will be true for you as well.

Two Stories

With thanks to Yann Martel.

(Genesis1:1, Matthew 5:3–10, John 15:13, Revelation 21:1–5)

Telling tips: This is one to tell on your own.

Here are two stories.
Which one do you prefer?

The first story begins like this:
Once upon a time, a very long time ago, there was a series of accidents. Energy and matter and molecules collided and somehow you are here today. Here by coincidence. Here by chance.

The second story starts this way:
In the beginning, God created the heavens and the earth. And you are here today, not by accident, but because he designed you, and loves you and wants to have a relationship with you.

Here are two stories.
Which one do you prefer?

The first story continues:

The fit live. The weak die. So kill or be killed. Survival is the name of the game. Look out for number one.

And here's how the second story goes:
Blessed are the meek. Blessed are the poor. Blessed are the peacemakers. Greater love has no one than this, that he lay down his life for his friends.

Here are two stories.
Which one do you prefer?

The first story finishes like this:
You die. The end.

And the second story? Actually, the second story has no end at all:
'Then I saw a new heaven and a new earth... There will be no more death or mourning or crying or pain, for the old order of things has passed away... I am making everything new!'

Here are two stories.
Two stories to explain the world.
No one can prove which one is true.
No scientist, no philosopher, no politician, no priest.
It's up to you to choose.
So here are two stories.
Which one do you prefer?

The Morning of the World

(Genesis 1–2)

Telling tips: Give the group sounds to make for each of the key phrases as below. For the animal noises section, you might even want to separate your audience into four groups, one for each kind of animal noise. Then let the sounds build on top of each other.

'It was clean.' (Make a happy 'Aaah!' sound.)

'It was quiet.' (Say 'Shhh'.)

'Make some noise!' (Do all of the animal sounds together: singing birds, splashing fish, buzzing insects, roaring beasts.)

'The first man, Adam.' (Yawn.)

Then lead the group in doing the appropriate sounds again at the end for the words 'quiet', 'clean', 'noisy' and 'Adam'.

What was it like on the morning of the world?
   It was clean.
   Clean as a baby, fresh from a bath.
   Clean as the tires on a brand new bicycle.
   Clean as a spring sunrise.
   Clean as a mountain snowfall.
   What was it like on the morning of the world?
   It was clean.

What was it like on the morning of the world?
   It was quiet.

Every now and then, a breeze would catch hold of a leaf and send it crashing against its neighbour. Or a stream would bubble and bounce against its banks.

But otherwise it was quiet.

Quiet as a sleeping baby.

Quiet as a coasting bicycle.

Quiet as the rising sun.

Quiet as the falling snow.

What was it like on the morning of the world?

It was quiet.

Maybe too quiet.

What was it like on the morning of the world?

It was time to make some noise!

So God spoke – that was the first noise. And a zoo of noises followed.

Singing birds.

Splashing fish.

Buzzing insects.

Roaring beasts.

And then a yawn from the first man, Adam.

'I've got something noisy for you to do,' God said to Adam.

And he gave him a job. The best kind of job there is. A job that is more like a game. And the game was called 'Name the Animals'!

What was it like on the morning of the world?

It was time to make some noise.

Adam looked. Adam listened. Where to start?

And then an animal dropped a nut on his head.

The animal was grey. It had small pointed ears. Its bristly tail was as long as its body. And it sat on a branch and chattered at Adam as if it were scolding him. What did Adam name it? Nobody knows.

14

But when the people who lived in Greece first saw it and noticed that its tail was as long as it body, they called it 'squirrel' – which means 'shadow tail'.

Again Adam looked. Again Adam listened.

Then Adam spotted another animal, shuffling towards him through the undergrowth.

This animal was half the size of Adam. It was covered with bright orange fur. It walked on its feet, like Adam did. And on its knuckles, like Adam didn't.

But the most remarkable thing about this animal was its face – a face that looked a bit like Adam's face, in fact.

What did Adam name it? Nobody knows.

But when the people who lived in Malaysia first saw this animal, walking through the forest with its sad man face, they called it 'orang-utan' – which means 'man of the woods'.

Once more Adam looked. Once more Adam listened.

And he heard a munching, crunching sound.

Adam turned round, and behind him there stood a creature twice his height, chewing the bark off a tree. It was shaggy and brown. It had four long, knobbly legs. And sticking out of its head were two branches like a pair of open hands.

What did Adam name it? Nobody knows.

But when the people who lived in North America first saw this huge, shaggy animal, they called it 'moose', which means 'he strips off bark'.

So Adam named the animals.

Nobody knows what he called them.

Nobody knows how long it took.

But when he was finished, Adam looked at the world.

It was no longer clean. Birds' nests filled the trees. Rabbit holes dotted the ground. Fish littered the streams. And there was hardly a leaf anywhere that hadn't been chewed or chomped or nibbled on.

Then Adam listened to the world.

It was no longer quiet.

The air was full of cawing and squawking and singing. The ground was crawling with snorting and grunting and squeaking. The streams were rushing with jumping and splashing and diving. And the jungle rustled and snapped and shook.

What was it like on the morning of the world?

The world was no longer quiet. The world was no longer clean.

It was noisy. And it was messy.

So God gave Adam a name for it.

And the name God gave it was 'Good'.

The Edge of the River

(Exodus 2:1–10)

Telling tips: Give your group a sound to make when they hear these words or phrases:

'Wet' (Say 'Ooh' with a drippy, shaking water from your hands or wringing water from a shirt motion.)

'Boring' (Make a big yawn.)

'Looking bad' (Say 'Uh-oh'.)

'Looking even worse' (Make a bigger 'Uh-oh' sound.)

'Looking better' (Say 'Phew!')

'Time to do something' (Look at watch.)

'Time to wonder' (Say 'Wow!')

What was it like at the edge of the river?

It was wet.

Squishy toe wet.

Soggy bottom wet.

Hot-and-muggy sweaty wet.

The girl peered through the reeds. They sprouted thick and tall from the riverbank mud.

The girl peered out onto the river at a bobbing bulrush boat. She hoped that her brother was, at least, dry.

What was it like at the edge of the river?

It was wet.

What was it like at the edge of the river?

It was boring.

She was supposed to watch her brother. That's what her mother had said. She was supposed to make sure that nothing happened to him. She was supposed to just sit there and wait.

But for how long?

Till Pharaoh, king of Egypt, decided to stop killing all the baby Hebrew boys? Till her little brother started to outgrow his bulrush boat? Till his arms poked through the sides, and his legs poked through the end, and his head popped out of the top?

The girl laughed when she thought of that. It was nice to laugh for a change. Better than being bored.

Better than sitting leg-stiff still.

Better than staring, eyes tired and sore.

Better than nodding off, eyelids drooping and chin dropping onto her chest.

What was it like at the edge of the river?

It was boring.

What was it like at the edge of the river?

It was looking bad.

The girl's long wait was broken by the sound of voices.

The river bank reeds were broken by tramping feet.

And the hot sweat of boredom broke into a cold sweaty fear.

The girl crouched down as low as she could, so she could see without being seen.

What she saw were women.

What she saw were Egyptian women.

What she saw were Egyptian women walking alongside the river, right towards her baby brother in his bulrush boat!

If they find him, she thought, they'll kill him.

But what could she do?

She was too small to fight them. She was too slow to reach him and pull him back to shore. And there was no time to run for help.

What was it like at the edge of the river?

It was looking bad.

What was it like at the edge of the river?

It was looking even worse!

The baby started to cry. The women started to point. And then one of them waded out into the river, pulled the bulrush boat out of the water and carried it back to shore.

The other women gathered round and blocked the girl's view. Now she was more helpless than ever!

And then the girl remembered. She remembered the stories her mother had told her about God.

God, who had led Abraham to a special land.

God, who had protected Jacob from the anger of his brother.

God, who had saved Joseph from another pharaoh's prison.

Maybe, just maybe, she thought, God could save her baby brother, too.

'Please, God,' she prayed, 'don't let them hurt him.'

At last, the women moved away and the girl could see her little brother again.

He wasn't dead.

He wasn't hurt.

He wasn't even crying.

In fact, one of the women was holding him and hugging him and stroking his head.

What was it like at the edge of the river?

It was looking better!

What was it like at the edge of the river?

It was time to do something.

If those Egyptian women were not going to hurt her brother, then the girl wanted to know what they did intend to do with him. So she crept towards them, her head below the reeds and her ears wide open.

'I am Pharaoh's daughter,' she heard one of the women say. 'I can do what I please. And what pleases me is to adopt this Hebrew child as my own. What I need is some woman to feed him and care for him until he is old enough to come and live with me.'

Like a pheasant spooked by a dog, like a puppet on a stage, like a Jack-in-the-box (or better still, a Jill-in-the-box!), the girl popped up out of the reeds.

'I know a woman,' she said, 'who would be just perfect for that job. She doesn't live far from here, and I am sure that she would love and care for your baby as if he were her very own!'

What was it like at the edge of the river?

It was time to do something.

What was it like at the edge of the river?

It was time to wonder.

'All right,' said the Egyptian to the girl. 'Go and fetch this woman. Say that Pharaoh's daughter commands her to care for...' And, here, she paused. 'For little "Pulled Out". For I pulled him out of the water!'

The girl nodded, then turned and ran quickly home.

How wonderful! Her brother was safe!

More wonderful still – his own mother would be able to care for him!

But what a silly name. Little 'Pulled Out'.

What was the Egyptian word for that? Moses.

And then, the girl thought, maybe it wasn't so silly. Maybe her brother's new name was a wonder, too. For hadn't she prayed? And hadn't the God of her fathers heard her prayer and pulled little Moses out of trouble? Like he'd pulled Abraham and Jacob and Joseph out of trouble, all those years ago?

God had pulled them out to do something special with them. And so the girl wondered. Had God pulled out Moses to do something special with him, as well?

What was it like at the edge of the river?

It was time to wonder.

Samson Was a Strong Man

(Judges 13–16)

Telling tips: This is mostly one to do on your own. You might like to get the crowd to do something with the 'hair just kept on growing' line. Maybe point to them and let them say it when you get there.

Samson was a strong man.

But he wasn't strong because he lifted weights.

And he wasn't strong because he did lots of press-ups.

And he wasn't strong because he had big muscles.

No, Samson was strong because his mother had promised God that he would never drink strong wine.

That he would never, ever drink strong beer.

And that he would never, ever, ever cut his hair.

And Samson had promised that, too.

Samson was strong because of God.

So, one day, God asked Samson to do a strong thing.

'The Philistines are hurting my people, Israel,' God said. 'And I want you to protect them.'

So that's what Samson did. Or at least tried to do. Because it's fair to say that what he really did was to make a great big nuisance of himself!

He killed a lion with his bare hands.

And his hair just kept on growing.

He caught 300 foxes, tied their tails together in pairs and jammed a fiery torch between the tails. (Do not try this at home!) Then he sent them running through the Philistines' fields to burn down all their crops.

And his hair just kept on growing.

He took the jawbone of a dead donkey and used it to kill a thousand Philistine soldiers.

And his hair just kept on growing.

And when the Philistines thought they had him surrounded, he tore the enormous doors off the city gates of Gaza and carried them to the top of a hill.

And his hair just kept on growing.

So the rulers of the Philistines went to have a chat with Samson's girlfriend, Delilah.

'If you can find the secret to his strength,' they said, 'each of us will give you a great big pile of silver!'

So Delilah tried. 'Samson, oh Samson,' she cooed. 'Please tell me the secret of your strength.'

Now Samson really fancied Delilah. It's even fair to say that he was in love with her. But he wasn't stupid. So he decided to play a little trick on her.

'Tie me up with seven fresh bowstrings,' he lied, 'and I will be as weak as any man.'

So that's what Delilah did. She hid some men in the next room, she tied up Samson with the fresh bow-strings. And then she cried, 'Samson, oh Samson, the Philistines are coming!'

The men burst through the door! Samson burst the bow-strings!

He chased the men away.

And his hair just kept on growing.

'Samson, oh Samson,' Delilah pouted. 'You lied to me and made me look a fool. Tell me, tell me please, the true secret of your strength.'

Samson liked this game, so he told her another lie.

'Tie me up with new ropes – ropes that have never been used – and I will be as weak as any man.'

So that's what Delilah did. She hid some men in the next room again, and she tied up Samson with new ropes. And then she cried, 'Samson, oh Samson! The Philistines are coming!'

The men burst through the door. Samson burst the ropes as if they were threads. He chased the men away.

And his hair just kept on growing.

'Samson, oh Samson,' Delilah whined. 'You lied to me again, and made me look a bigger fool. Please, please, tell me the secret of your strength.'

Samson grinned. 'All right then,' he said. But it was just another lie. 'Take the seven braids of my hair and weave them into the cloth on your loom. And then I will be as weak as any man.'

So that's what Delilah did. She hid some more men in the next room. She wove Samson's seven long braids into the cloth on her loom. And then she cried, 'Samson, oh Samson, the Philistines are coming!'

The men burst through the door. Samson burst to his feet, loom and cloth and all. He chased the men away.

And his hair just kept on growing.

'Samson, oh Samson,' wept Delilah. 'You don't love me at all! This is the third time you've made me look a fool. Please, please, please, please, pretty please tell me the secret of your strength.' And she said this not once, not twice, but day after day after day.

Maybe it was the nagging. Maybe it was the tears. Maybe Samson was truly, deeply in love with Delilah. Or maybe Samson just forgot where his strength really came from. Maybe he thought it was all down to him – and not the God he'd made his promise to.

Whatever the reason, Samson finally told Delilah the truth.

'I made a promise once,' he said, 'that a razor would never touch my head. Cut my hair and I will be as weak as any man.'

So that's what Delilah did. She hid some men in the next room – the rulers of the Philistines this time. And when Samson fell asleep, she had one of the men cut off his seven long braids.

'Samson, oh Samson!' she cried. 'The Philistines are coming!'

Samson woke. 'I'll chase them away, just like before!' he boasted. But when the men burst through the door, Samson could do nothing. He really was as weak as any man.

So the Philistines grabbed him, poked out his eyes, bound him and carried him off to prison. They chained him to a great stone wheel, and day after day, he pushed the wheel to grind their corn.

And his hair just kept on growing.

Some time later, the Philistines decided to have a big party – to celebrate Samson's capture and to thank their god Dagon for delivering him into their hands. What they didn't count on was the true God coming to their party – the God of Israel. The God who had given Samson his strength and who still wanted to use him to protect his people.

Three thousand Philistines and more gathered in the temple on that day. The place was packed. And in the middle of the celebration, the rulers had Samson dragged into their midst. The people laughed and clapped when they saw him.

'Our god has beaten our enemy,' they cheered, 'the one who caused us so much trouble.'

And when they were done laughing, Samson was dragged to the side of the temple and stood among the pillars.

'You know I'm blind,' said Samson to the man who guarded him. 'Put me where I can feel the pillars, please, so I can lean against them.'

So that's what the servant did. He put Samson between the pillars – the pillars that supported the whole of the temple.

'Dear Lord,' prayed Samson, 'the only strength I ever had came from you. I remember that now, so I ask that you would remember me and give me that strength just one more time.'

And with his left hand on one pillar and his right hand on another, he began to push.

The pillars creaked. The pillars cracked. The pillars crumbled. The pillars collapsed. And when they did, the whole of the temple came crashing down with them. It crashed down on the people. It crashed down on the rulers. And it crashed down on Samson, too.

'Let me die with the Philistines!' cried Samson. And so he did, killing many more with his death than he had ever done in his life, and doing finally what God had asked him to do – protecting his people from their enemy.

A Tale of Two Families

(1 Samuel 1–2)

Telling tips: This is one to tell on your own.

Hannah

Hannah was barren. And in the time and the place that Hannah lived, to be barren was to be cursed.

But things are not always what they look like.

Situations are not always what they seem.

And God has a way of taking one thing and turning it into something completely different.

Hannah was married to Elkanah – a man of means who could afford a second wife – Peninnah. And Peninnah, as it happens, was not barren at all. She had a brood of children, whom she stood before Hannah, at every opportunity, to make her curse even worse.

Elkanah was a good man. He saw, he understood, he longed to ease Hannah's pain. So when the family trooped from their home in Ramah to the holy place at Shiloh each year, and when they sat down to eat a portion of the meat that had been offered as a sacrifice to God, Elkanah always made sure that Hannah got a double helping of that meat – a special treat – and, surely, the first recorded example of comfort eating.

In spite of all her children, however (and as a powerful argument for monogamy!), Peninnah was jealous of this simple act of kindness.

And she did all she could to make that a curse, as well.

'It is God who has closed your womb,' she would tell Hannah, there, in the presence of God himself, in his own holy place. And she would do this, not once, not twice, but again and again and again, right up to the time of the feast. And poor Hannah would be so upset that she could not enjoy the treat her husband had planned for her. In fact, she could not eat at all.

'Eat, Hannah, eat!' Elkanah would say. He meant well, but (being a man!) he ended up saying all the things a husband should never say to his wife when she is so unhappy she can't eat.

'Why are you crying?

Why are you so upset?

You may not have any children – but you have me!'

One year, Hannah was so upset that she left the table altogether. She went to the door of the holy place, where Eli the priest was sitting. And there, through her tears, she offered up a prayer to God.

'Look at me, Lord, please! See my misery. Remember my condition. And give me a son, I pray. For if you do, then I will give him back to you, and dedicate him as your servant for all the days of his life.'

These words were hard words. So hard that she could not speak them out loud. Hannah's lips moved, her tears flowed, and the old priest Eli (another man!) assumed that she was drunk.

'Sober up, woman!' he said. 'This is neither the time nor the place. Take your bottle and go home!'

Hannah could not believe this. All she wanted was help, and here was another curse.

'Drunk?' she cried. 'Is that what you think? I'm not drunk! In fact, I can hardly eat or drink a thing! I'm here to pray – that's all – to pour out my grief and my troubles before the Lord.'

'I see,' said Eli, sorry not only for her sadness but for his mistake. 'Then go in peace. And may the God of Israel give you what you asked for.'

It was a blessing. A blessing, at last. Hard won, to be sure. But a blessing and not a curse.

So Hannah went.

And Hannah had something to eat.

And when she saw her husband, she smiled.

And when they returned to Ramah, she lay with him and conceived and gave birth to a son and called him Samuel – a name which means 'God heard me.'

And when Samuel was old enough, she took him back to Shiloh, back to the old priest Eli.

And though it sounds like the act of a crazy woman, or a woman who has had too much to drink, she left her only son there to serve in the holy place.

A blessing in return for a blessing.

A blessing, not a curse.

Eli

Eli was a priest – the son of the son of the son of the son (and a few more sons!) of Moses' own brother, Aaron. And at the time that Eli lived, to be a priest – a chosen mediator between God and man – was to be blessed.

But things are not always what they look like.

Situations are not always what they seem.

And sadly we all have a way of taking one thing and making it into something completely different.

Eli had two sons – Hophni and Phinehas.

And the Bible says it about as plainly as it can be said.

Eli's sons were wicked men; they had no regard for the Lord.

(Not the best of qualifications for the priesthood!)

They had a plan, these brothers – a clever scam – and it went something like this. When the people sacrificed their animals to God, just some of the meat was burned on the altar. Only the best bits were offered up to the Lord. To put it in contemporary terms, if you were offering God a Bourbon crème, he would get to lick out the stuff in the middle. If you were offering him a piece of cake, he would get the corner with all the icing and the big sugar rose. Well, at the time of our story, the best bits were the fatty bits. Those bits were offered to God. And the rest of the meat was put into a pot and boiled.

During this process one of the priest's servants was supposed to plunge a fork into the pot and fish out whatever piece of meat the fork found. This piece was given to the priests to eat – a potluck way of providing for their needs.

But Hophni and Phinehas were not satisfied with this potluck blessing. They were tired of their servants hooking the odd neck and hoof and kneebone along with the choicer cuts. And what is more, without regard for their obligation to God (or to the possibility of rising cholesterol and accompanying heart disease), they were keen to add a little more fat to their diet.

So they ordered their servants to approach the worshippers before the sacrifices were made.

'The priests do not want boiled meat,' they would say. 'They want to choose their piece now, while the meat is raw.'

And if the worshippers objected and said, 'Well at least let us burn the fat for God first,' then all sorts of nasty things were likely to happen to them.

Word of this spread among the people. And finally old Eli, who should have been keeping an eye on his sons, heard about it too.

To be fair, he told them off in no uncertain terms.

'If you sin against another man,' he said, 'God is there to intervene for you. But who will be there to help you when you sin against God himself?'

But Hophni and Phinehas were enjoying their position and its newly found privileges, and refused to change their ways.

So God sent a prophet to Eli, who gave him some unhappy news. 'You have been so blessed,' the prophet said. 'God has chosen you and your family to make offerings and burn incense and to be his priests. But now you have dishonoured him by taking for yourself what is rightfully his. And so the Lord says that there will no longer be old men in your family. Your sons will die together, on the same day, and the priesthood will be given to another.'

And that's exactly what happened. Hophni and Phinehas were killed in a battle with the Philistines over the Ark of the Covenant. Killed on the same day. And when he was given the news, old Eli was so shaken that he fell off his chair, broke his neck and died.

And what should have been a blessing – a blessing to the people, a blessing to God, a blessing to Eli and his sons – became a curse.

For while God is more than able to turn a curse into a blessing, only we can find a way to turn a blessing into a curse.

The Middle of the Night

(1 Samuel 3)

Telling tips: Give the group something to say when they hear each of these phrases in the story.
'Hard to sleep' (Yawn.)
'Like a dream' (Say 'Oooh', in a sleepy, dreamy tone.)
'Embarrassing' (Say 'Oh, dear.')
'Kind of creepy' (Make a mildly scared noise.)
'Nightmare' (Make a very scared noise.)
'Amazing' (Say 'Wow!')

What was is like, in the middle of the night?

It was hard to sleep.

Lamplight bounced off the Ark of the Covenant – the big box where God was supposed to live – and tossed strange shadows on the thin tent walls.

Those shadows bounced around inside young Samuel's head and tossed strange pictures into his dreams. And the dreams kept him bouncing and tossing on his bed.

What was it like, in the middle of the night?

It was hard to sleep.

What was it like, in the middle of the night?

It was like a dream. 'Samuel!' called a voice. And the boy's eyes cracked open at the sound of his name. Was it a dream, or had he really heard it?

'Samuel!' called the voice again.

And the boy thought, It must be my master, Eli.

Old, weak and blind, Eli the priest often needed Samuel's help. So the boy climbed out of bed, adding his shadow to the shadows on the wall. And by the light of one flickering lamp, he stumbled towards old Eli's room.

What was it like, in the middle of the night?

It was like a dream.

What was it like, in the middle of the night?

It was embarrassing.

Samuel tapped Eli on the shoulder and whispered his name. The old man grunted and rolled over. Samuel tapped him harder. The old man grunted again. So Samuel grabbed his shoulder and shook him. And the old man coughed and woke and grabbed the boy's arm.

'Samuel? Is that you? What do you want?'

Samuel was confused. 'I don't want anything. You called me and here I am.'

The old man sighed and shut his eyes.

'I didn't call you. You must have been dreaming. Go back to bed.'

So Samuel went. But as he made his way past the Ark of the Covenant, he couldn't help feeling a little foolish for disturbing the old priest.

What was it like, in the middle of the night?

It was embarrassing.

What was it like, in the middle of the night?

It was getting kind of creepy.

The boy had hardly shut his eyes when he heard the voice call 'Samuel!' once again.

Surely it was Eli, this time. So Samuel raced back to his master.

'I'm here!' the boy shouted, surprising even himself with the volume.

Eli woke up. But he didn't ask who it was this time. He didn't even roll over. He just blinked his weak eyes and said ever so sternly, 'I did not call you. I do not need you. Go back to bed!'

So Samuel crept back to his room, shaking his head and fighting the shivers that were starting to climb up the middle of his back.

What was it like, in the middle of the night?

It was getting kind of creepy.

What was it like, in the middle of the night?

It was like a nightmare.

The boy jumped into bed and pulled the cover over his face. But the cover was thin, and through it he could still see the light from the flickering lamp. And the shadow of the Ark on the wall.

So he shut his eyes. He shut them tight. But shutting his eyes could not shut out his fear. Samuel could still hear his pounding heart and, when it finally came, the sound of that voice as well.

'Samuel! Samuel!' the voice called.

And Samuel knew what he had to do. He didn't care what the old priest said. Nothing was going to make him stay in that place. Nothing!

So he ran to Eli's room, not daring to look at anything along the way.

What was it like in the middle of the night?

It was like a nightmare!

When Samuel reached Eli's room, he found the old priest wide awake, sitting up in bed. He threw himself into Eli's arms and buried his head in the priest's chest.

Eli held him tight until he stopped shaking, but he said nothing at all. He just peered into the darkness with his weak old eyes. And then, suddenly, those eyes began to shine – as if they saw something, as if they recognized someone.

'Samuel,' he said gently, 'I did not call you. But I think I know who did. If I am not mistaken, it was the Lord God, himself.'

'You mean the one who lives in the box?' whispered Samuel.

Eli smiled. 'The Lord God does not live in the box,' he explained. 'The Lord God cannot fit into any box. But he gave us the box to remind us that he is always with us. And he told our ancestors to put things in the box to remind us that he cares for us and that he has spoken to us. He has not spoken for a long time, Samuel, but I believe that he wants to speak to you tonight.'

Samuel looked at Eli. 'So what should I do?'

'You must go back to your room and lie down,' said the priest, 'and if he calls you again, you must say, "Speak, Lord, for I am your servant, and I am ready to listen."'

What was it like in the middle of the night?

It was frightening – and amazing – all at the same time.

Samuel walked slowly back to his room. He kept one trembling hand against the wall, and the other he spread, like a fan, across his eyes, so he could just see through his fingers.

When Samuel looked into his room, everything seemed normal. But as soon as he entered it, everything began to change. The light from the flickering lamp grew brighter. The shadows got darker. And through the tent walls, above the Ark of the Covenant, Samuel saw the shape of a figure.

The figure was frightening, and Samuel wanted to shut his fingers. But the figure was strangely beautiful, too, so Samuel also wanted to look.

Then, in the same voice he'd heard before, the figure called Samuel's name.

'Speak, Lord,' whispered Samuel, trying hard to remember what Eli had told him. 'I am your servant, and I am ready to listen.'

So the Lord spoke – and that was the first of many times that he had a message for Samuel.

Samuel listened – and that was the first of many times that this prophet heard the voice of the Lord.

What was it like, in the middle of the night?

It was frightening – and amazing – all at the same time.

Elijah Number One

(1 Kings 17)

Telling tips: This telling is built around Robin Mark's song, 'Days of Elijah'. So you will need a guitar (preferably – although a keyboard will also do) to keep the beat of the song in the background in the key of B flat. When you get to the chorus, simply sing the line 'These are the days of Elijah' twice. And then carry on reading the next verse of the story. I let the crowd repeat each line in the verse, so you might want to put the text onto a screen, so people can read the words. At the very end of the story, I usually lead the crowd in the whole of the song itself.

If you do not have musical accompaniment available, or if you don't know the song, you can just read the story. Keep a good rhythm, and let the crowd join with you in saying 'These are the days of Elijah'. Robin Mark's song is available through Daybreak Music Ltd.

Chorus:

These are the days of Elijah.
These are the days of Elijah.

There once was a prophet called Elijah,
And he told the king
That the rain would stop
'Cause the people had wandered from the Lord.

There once was a prophet called Elijah,
Who ran and hid
'Cause the king was angry,
And the ravens brought him bread and meat.

Chorus:

These are the days of Elijah.
These are the days of Elijah.

There once was a prophet called Elijah,
Who met a widow
And asked for bread,
Though her oil and wheat were nearly gone.

'Have faith,' said the prophet called Elijah.
And the more she used,
The more she had,
And her oil and wheat were never gone!

Chorus:

These are the days of Elijah.
These are the days of Elijah.

There once was a prophet called Elijah,
And the widow's son
Fell ill and died,
And she blamed the prophet for his death.

'Have faith,' said the prophet called Elijah.
And he comforted the mother,
And he prayed for the son,
And the boy came back to life!

Chorus:

These are the days of Elijah.
These are the days of Elijah.

So God called a prophet named Elijah,
And he calls us, too,
To go out in the world
And to stand and speak for what's true.

Chorus:

These are the days of Elijah.
These are the days of Elijah.

Elijah Number Two

(1 Kings 18)

Telling tips: See 'Elijah Number One'. As you will see, the last verse is longer than the rest. Keep the rhythm and repetition going and make each line louder and stronger than the one before.

Chorus:

These are the days of Elijah.
These are the days of Elijah.

There once was a prophet called Elijah,
Who challenged the king
To a contest on Mount Carmel
To see whose god was really real.

'Here's the deal,' said the prophet called Elijah.
'You build an altar,
I'll build one, too,
And we'll see whose god provides the fire.'

Chorus:

These are the days of Elijah.
These are the days of Elijah.

'I'll call my prophets,' said the king to Elijah.
'Four hundred here,
Four-fifty there –
You're outnumbered. You won't stand a chance.'

'Bring it on!' said the prophet called Elijah.
'Nine hundred prophets of Baal
Against one prophet of the Lord.
I figure that's just about fair.'

Chorus:

These are the days of Elijah.
These are the days of Elijah.

'You go first,' said the prophet called Elijah.
So the prophets built their altar.
And they stacked up their wood.
And they waited for Baal to burn their bulls.

'Nothing's happened,' said the prophet called Elijah.
So the prophets danced.
And the prophets prayed.
From breakfast time to dinner time and more.

Chorus:

These are the days of Elijah.
These are the days of Elijah.

'What's the matter?' asked the prophet called Elijah.
'Is your god asleep?
Is he hard of hearing?
Or maybe he's just sitting on the loo.

'Still nothing's happened,' said the prophet called Elijah.
So the prophets shouted
And threw themselves about.
From dinner time to tea-time and more.

Chorus:

These are the days of Elijah.
These are the days of Elijah.

'Now it's my turn,' said the prophet called Elijah.
And he built an altar,
And he stacked up the wood,
And then he added one final touch.

'Bring me water!' said the prophet called Elijah.
And he dumped it on the altar,
And he dumped it on the wood,
Until everything was soggy and wet.

Chorus:

These are the days of Elijah.
These are the days of Elijah.

'Help me, Lord!' prayed the prophet called Elijah.
'Send fire from heaven.
Show your power to the people
So they'll turn back and call you God again.'

So the Lord heard the prophet called Elijah.
And he burned up the bull,
And he burned up the wood,
And he burned up the stones,

40

And he burned up the soil,
And he boiled the water,
And sent it steaming to the sky,
And the people bowed and called him God again.
And the people bowed and called him God again.
And the people bowed and called him God again.

Chorus:

These are the days of Elijah.
These are the days of Elijah.

Elijah Number Three

(1 Kings 19)

Telling tips: See 'Elijah Number One'. In the 'still small voice'
line keep the rhythm and make the line 'stiller and smaller' each
time.

Chorus:

These are the days of Elijah.
These are the days of Elijah.

There once was a prophet called Elijah.
The queen wanted to kill him
'Cause he'd beaten the Baals,
So God sent an angel to his side.

Now the angel made a cake for Elijah –
It was an angel sort of cake
From a chef sort of fella,
Like Ainsley or Jamie or Nigella.

Chorus:

These are the days of Elijah.
These are the days of Elijah.

'I'm all alone!' cried the prophet called Elijah
'I've done my best,
But I'm all that's left,
And I just want to run away and die.'

'Go to the mountain,' said God to Elijah,
'And wait for me to pass,
And wait for me to speak,
And I'll tell you everything you need to know.'

Chorus:

These are the days of Elijah.
These are the days of Elijah.

So to the mountain went the prophet called Elijah.
And the wind blew hard,
And the earth shook harder,
And a fire lit up the sky.

Then God spoke to the prophet called Elijah.
But he wasn't in the wind,
And he wasn't in the earthquake,
And he wasn't in the fire.
But he was there in the still small voice.
But he was there in the still small voice.
But he was there in the still small voice.
But he was there in the still small voice.

Chorus:

These are the days of Elijah.
These are the days of Elijah.

And God said to the prophet called Elijah,
'You're not alone,
You never were.
There are seven thousand just like you!'

'Seven thousand?' cried the prophet called Elijah.
'Then I'm not alone,
I'm not afraid.'
And he went off to do the work of the Lord.

Chorus:

These are the days of Elijah.
These are the days of Elijah.

Songs in Search of a Tune:
Shout Your Name

(Psalm 148)

**Telling tips: I like music. I like it a lot. And I've always wanted
to write songs. So I sat down this past year and wrote some lyrics.
The problem is that I'm not very good at the tune side of things.
So we'll just call these pieces 'poems', which you can use as they
stand, but which also might lend themselves to having music added
by someone who knows something about such things!**

I wrote this one as a kind of modern 'All Creatures of Our God and
King' where all creation is called to praise the Lord. There are
two obvious differences, however. First of all, 'All Creatures of
Our God and King' is much better. And secondly, I wanted to
make my song personal, so the names in the song are all people in
the church I pastor. I'm sure they wouldn't mind you using their
names, too. And, who knows, you might have a Rex and a Marlene
and an Alan and a Paul in your church, as well. But if your Stan
and Margaret shouldn't really be holding hands, for example, that
verse might be just a bit embarrassing and result in lots of
unwanted pastoral issues. Therefore, I suggest that you might like
to substitute the names of people that you know into the song. Be
warned, however, that it's very difficult to find words that rhyme
with Nigel.

Verse 1:

Novas and northern lights,
Sea lions, stalagmites,
Saturn and Mars and fish shaped like stars
Shout your name,
Shout your name.

Sunsets and snowstorms,
Single-celled life forms,
Photons and protons and goats on the hill
Shout your name,
Shout your name.

Bridge:

And Rex and Marlene,
And the girl dressed in green,
And the lad in between
Want to shout,
Want to shout your name, too.

And Wendy and Paul,
At the back of the hall,
And Allan who's tall
Want to shout,
Want to shout your name, too.

Chorus:

And they shout, 'Maker!'
And they shout, 'Earth Shaker!'
And they shout, 'Death Breaker!'
And they shout, 'God!'

Verse 2:

Peacocks and polar bears,
Sand dunes and solar flares,
Grass snakes and corncrakes and cold mountain lakes
Shout your name,
Shout your name.

Cherubs and chimpanzees,
Bull rushes, bumble-bees,
Antelopes, cantaloupes, pastors and popes
Shout your name,
Shout your name.

Bridge:

And Rex and Marlene,
And the girl dressed in green,
And the lad in between
Want to shout,
Want to shout your name, too.

And Margaret and Stan,
Who are still holding hands,
And the guys in the band
Want to shout,
Want to shout your name, too.

Chorus:

And they shout, 'Maker!'
And they shout, 'Earth Shaker!'
And they shout, 'Death Breaker!'
And they shout, 'God!'

The Passion

(Isaiah 53:5)

Telling tips: You might want to read the passage from Isaiah out loud before you do this reading.

When I was six, I spilled my milk. And it poured over my plate, and onto my lap and down to the floor. So my mother soaked up the milk, and mopped up the floor, and stopped me from crying and popped me into a fresh set of clothes. And when she finally got back to the table, her dinner was cold.

> *When the milk gets spilled, somebody needs to clean it up.*
> *And cleaning up means giving up something for someone else.*

I turned on the evening news and there was a house on fire. No one knew how the fire started. Arson? Faulty wiring? A stray, smouldering cigarette? But everyone knew that there was an old woman trapped in that house. So a fireman went in and carried her out. And there he sat, sooty and sweaty and sucking down oxygen.

> *When the milk gets spilled, somebody needs to clean it up.*
> *When the fire burns, somebody needs to put it out.*
> *And putting it out means putting yourself at risk for someone else.*

I watched *The Passion of the Christ* when it first came out. I sat through two hours of violence and pain. And I asked myself, 'Why? Why did Jesus have to die that way?'

Then I thought about my mother. And I thought about the fireman. And I thought about this world of ours, where people get knocked down and blood gets spilled and hatred burns. And I wondered, If it takes the sacrifice of a mum to mop up milk, and the sacrifice of a fireman to put out a fire, maybe, just maybe, nothing less than the sacrifice of God himself is adequate to clean up the whole of this mess of a world.

When the milk gets spilled, somebody needs to clean it up.
When the fire burns, somebody needs to put it out.
When the world goes wrong, somebody needs to fix it.
And fixing it up means God giving himself up for us.

The Boys Who Liked to Say NO!

(Daniel 1)

Telling tips: NO! is the operative word in this story. So NO! is at the heart of the participation device, as well. Tell your group that they are to say NO! every time it comes up in the story. Tell them to get louder and more determined each time. Tell them you'd like a real full-blooded rebellion here. And then have a great time!

You might also like to divide the crowd into three or four groups and ask them to do different kinds of NO!s. In a high voice, low voice, soft voice or silly voice, perhaps.

When the boys lived in Jerusalem, their Hebrew friends knew them as Daniel, Hananiah, Mishael and Azariah.

When Jerusalem was conquered, and they were taken as captives to the palace of King Nebuchadnezzar, they were given Babylonian names. And everyone knew them as Belteshazzar, Shadrach, Meshach and Abednego.

But anyone who knew them well, simply knew them as The Boys Who Liked to Say NO!

They were handsome, these boys. And clever and strong, to boot. Sons of Jerusalem's most important families. So Nebuchadnezzar decided to treat them well. He gave them soft beds to sleep on, rich food to eat and an education at his very best university – all in the hope that they would forget about Jerusalem and learn to call Babylon 'home'. And that the rest of their captured people would, too.

But Nebuchadnezzar hadn't reckoned on them being The Boys Who Liked to Say NO!

One of King Nebuchadnezzar's servants was an enormous man named Ashpenaz. He had a big belly and a bald head, and more than anything else in the world, he liked to eat! So he was put in charge of turning The Boys Who Liked to Say NO! into good Babylonians.

'For dinner tonight,' he announced, 'you will have the following choices from the king's own menu:

Pink pork sausages.

Plump pork chops.

Or my own personal favourite – Mrs Puffy's Perfect Pork Pies!'

Ashpenaz wiped the corners of his mouth with the back of his chubby hand. The thought of all those pork products made him quiver with joy. But The Boys Who Liked to Say NO! were calm. They knew exactly what to do.

The king's food looked good, and smelled even better, but they knew it was made from something their Law said they could not eat. The Law they had learned in Jerusalem. The Law their God had given them. The Law and the city and the God they were determined never to forget.

So they turned to Ashpenaz and together they said, 'NO!'

Ashpenaz could not believe it.

'No pink pork sausages?' he asked.

'NO!' said Shadrach. 'But I wouldn't mind a few carrots.'

'No plump pork chops?'

'NO!' said Meshach. 'I'll just have a green salad.'

'And not even one of Mrs Puffy's Perfect Pork Pies?'

'NO!' said Abednego. 'But a roast potato would be lovely.'

Ashpenaz wiped the sweat from his forehead.

'The king will be very angry,' he explained. 'If you do not eat this food, you will grow tired and ill. And then there is no telling what the king will do to me. He may throw me in prison, or torture me, or cut me up into tiny little pieces. Or worse still, take away my daily ration of bacon butties. Please, won't you reconsider!'

'NO!' said Daniel. 'But we promise you that you will not get into trouble. For we will not grow tired and ill. Tell the king to put us to the test. For ten days, the four of us will have nothing but vegetables and water. The other boys in the palace can eat your food. At the end of that time, we shall see who looks more fit.'

Ashpenaz agreed, and so did the king, so for ten days, The Boys Who Liked to Say NO! said NO! to everything but vegetables and water – while the other boys ate their fill of pork sausages and pork chops and pork pies.

What happened? The God that Daniel, Shadrach, Meshach and Abednego would not forget did not forget them either! At the end of the test, The Boys Who Liked to Say NO! looked healthy and strong. And the other boys? Well, their bellies were bloated, their breath was bad, and I can't begin to tell you how they reacted when they discovered what was IN Mrs Puffy's Pork Pies!

So from then on, Daniel, Shadrach, Meshach and Abednego were allowed to eat whatever they liked. And even the king had to admit that they were both healthier and wiser than the rest. All because they were loyal to their God. And because they were The Boys Who Liked to Say NO!

King Nebuchadnezzar's First Dream

(Daniel 2)

Telling tips: I think the statue is the best place to bring in participation. Divide your group into six sections, one for each of the materials used in the statue. The Gold section will say 'Aaah!' The Silver section will say 'Oooh!' The Bronze section can tickle each other and say 'Cootchie-cootchie-coo!' The Iron section can stomp their feet. And the Iron and Clay section can shout 'Cracking Toast, Grommit!' (It's a stretch I know, so feel free to come up with an alternative.) The last group is the Rock group, and they could just shout 'the Rock!' in a big, growly voice.

Explain to them that they will do their bit every time they hear the name of their section used in the story. You will need to make sure you emphasize these words as you tell the story.

King Nebuchadnezzar had a dream.

A bad dream.

A troubling dream.

A dream that kept him up all night.

So he called together all his wise men – his magicians and enchanters, his sorcerers and astrologers.

'I have had a troubling dream,' he said. 'And I want you to tell me what it means.'

'No problem, your majesty,' grinned the wise men. 'Tell us your dream and we will tell you what it means.'

'Ah, but there is a problem,' said the king. 'If I told you my dream, you could make up any old rubbish to explain it. How would I know you were telling me the truth? So I have decided to set you a test. Pass, and you will receive a great reward. Fail, and I will chop you up into tiny little pieces.'

'And what kind of test would that be?' asked the wise men, not nearly so confident now.

'Tell me what my dream means,' said the king. 'But first, tell me what I dreamed!'

The wise men looked at each and trembled. No one had ever asked them to do this before.

'Seriously, your majesty,' they said at last, 'tell us your dream, and we'll tell you what it means.'

'I'm very serious,' said the king. 'And you're just stalling for time. You say you're wise. You say you're powerful. Then show me. Tell me what I dreamed, and then I will know for sure that you can tell me what it means.'

'But majesty,' stammered the wise men, every one of them trembling now. 'This is impossible. No one but the gods could do what you ask!'

King Nebuchadnezzar was furious, and declared that every wise man in Babylon should be chopped up into tiny little pieces. And so it was that the king's soldiers came looking for the wise man Daniel and his three wise friends – Shadrach, Meshach and Abednego.

Daniel did not tremble. No, he spoke to the soldier. He found out what the fuss was all about. He asked the king for just a little more time. And then he got together with his three friends – and had a prayer meeting!

They asked God to show them the king's dream. And when God did, Daniel went straight to Nebuchadnezzar.

'Do not chop the wise men into tiny little pieces,' he begged, 'for I can tell you what your dream means.'

'But can you tell me what I dreamed?' asked the king.

'I can't,' admitted Daniel. 'And neither can any other wise man or magician. But there is a God in heaven who can. He has shown me your dream, King Nebuchadnezzar. And now I will tell it to you.

'You saw a statue, your majesty – a giant statue!
  Its head was made of gold.
  Its chest and arms, of silver.
  Its belly and thighs were made of bronze.
  Its legs, of iron.
  And its feet were part iron and part clay.

'And then you saw a rock. A rock cut out of the hills, but not by human hands. The rock struck the statue on its feet of iron and clay and the statue broke into tiny little pieces that were swept away on the wind. But the rock? The rock grew into a mountain and filled the whole earth!'

Nebuchadnezzar was amazed. Daniel was right – down to the last detail. But before he could say anything, Daniel continued:

'That was your dream, O King. And here is what it means.

'Your kingdom is the head of gold. The kingdom to follow will not be quite as powerful as yours. That is the arms and chest of silver. The kingdom after that – the belly and thighs of bronze – will be less powerful still. But then will come another kingdom – the legs of iron – that will crush all before it. That kingdom will divide – the feet made of iron and clay – and in the days of that kingdom, the God of heaven will set up a kingdom of his own – the rock – that will never be destroyed.

'God has shown you the future, your majesty – that is the meaning of your dream!'

King Nebuchadnezzar said nothing at first. He fell to the floor and bowed before Daniel. Then he exclaimed:

'Daniel, your God is the God of gods,
The Lord whose wisdom never ceases.
He showed me the meaning of my dream
And now no one shall be chopped up into tiny little pieces!'

Songs in Search of a Tune:
Praise to our God

(Daniel 2:20–23)

Telling tips: Another one for you to do on your own. This song is taken from the prayer that Daniel prayed when he asked God to show him the meaning of King Nebuchadnezzar's dream.

Praise to our God for ever and ever,
Wisdom and power are his alone.
Praise to our God for ever and ever,
Wisdom and power are his alone.

He sets up the seasons – winter, spring, summer.
He knocks down the king – right off his throne.
He shines like a light into all that is hidden
And makes the deep, darkest mysteries known.

Praise to our God for ever and ever,
Wisdom and power are his alone.
Praise to our God for ever and ever,
Wisdom and power are his alone.

We praise you and thank you, O God of our fathers,
For all of the mercy that you have shown,

For sharing your wisdom and sharing your power
And making the secret things of kings known.

Praise to our God for ever and ever,
Wisdom and power are his alone.
Praise to our God for ever and ever,
Wisdom and power are his alone.

The Men Who Liked to Say NO!

(Daniel 3)

Telling tips: Again, as in 'The Boys Who Liked to Say NO!',
NO! is the operative word. It might be fun to divide the crowd
into four groups, one for Shadrach, one for Meshach, one for
Abednego and one for Nebuchadnezzar. Let each of the first
three do NO! in a different way and let the Nebuchadnezzar
group growl – GRRR! You may need to point to the appropriate
groups to let them know when to do their parts. All three of the
NO! groups can do the NO!s together when there is not a specific
speaker named.

One day, King Nebuchadnezzar's herald made an important
announcement:
'All prefects and satraps,
All magistrates and judges,
All councillors and governors,
All big shots and hobnobs,
Must report immediately to the Plain of Dura.
King Nebuchadnezzar has a surprise for you!'

When the officials got there, they found a golden statue, three
metres wide and thirty metres tall. It was the biggest statue they
had ever seen. And gathered around the bottom of the statue
was the biggest band they had ever heard.

The herald cleared his throat and took a deep breath:
'People of all nations and stations and languages,
People of all places and races and climes,
People of all landscapes and body shapes and backgrounds,
People of all time zones and hormones and kinds,
At the sound of
The trumpet, the trigon, the horn and the bagpipe,
The oboe, the zither, the harp and the lyre,
The wahoo, the farney, the honk and the oompah,
All of you must bow down and worship this golden statue.
And anyone who does not will be thrown into
A hot and humid, bright and blazing, flaming fiery furnace!'

While the herald caught his breath, King Nebuchadnezzar gave the signal and the band began to play. At once, everyone fell down and worshipped the statue.

Well, almost everyone.

For there were three officials, standing at the back, who did not bow down and who did not worship the statue. Shadrach, Meshach and Abednego. They were all grown up now – the *MEN* Who Liked to Say NO!

Now, most people knew King Nebuchadnezzar as the great and powerful ruler of Babylon. But anyone who knew him well, knew him simply as The King Who Liked to Say GRRR!

And when he saw the three men standing at the back, that is exactly what he did.

'GRRR!' he snarled. 'Who dares defy my order?'

'GRRR!' he growled. 'Who dares insult my god?'

'GRRR!' he roared. (For he was good at this!) 'Who dares? Who dares? Who dares?'

As it happened, there were several satraps and big shots and hobnobs nearby – native Babylonians, who didn't much like the idea of these foreigners from Jerusalem having such important jobs – who knew exactly who dared.

'Their names are Shadrach, Meshach and Abednego,' they told the king.

'GRRR!' snarled Nebuchadnezzar.. 'Bring them to me at once!'

'Well,' snapped the king, when the men were brought before him, 'you heard the order and failed to obey. Will you worship the statue now?'

'NO!' said Shadrach. 'We will not worship your idol. Our God has told us that would be wrong.'

'NO!' said Meshach. 'And we will not forget our God, or his Law, or the land he gave us – the land from which we were taken.'

'NO!' said Abednego, 'And we believe that our God will not forget us!'

'Then off to the furnace!' roared the king.

Nebuchadnezzar GRRR-ed all the way to the furnace.

'Make it hot!' he growled. 'Seven times hotter than it's been before. And tie them up tight, so there is no chance for escape!'

And so, tightly bound, The Men Who Liked to Say NO! were thrown into the furnace. But the flames were so hot that the men who threw them in died immediately!

'Charred. Sizzled. Burned to a crisp,' noted the herald.

Things were different, however, for Shadrach, Meshach and Abednego. They weren't burning. They weren't boiling. They weren't even sweating. And they weren't alone.

They could just make him out, moving through the fire. A flash of orange hair. Flaming red fingers. And a pair of burning eyes. The angel flickered like the flames before them, now red and orange, now yellow, now white. Then, one by one, he touched a finger to the ropes that bound them, and they smoked and sizzled and burned right through. But there was not so much as a blister on the skin of Shadrach, Meshach and Abednego.

'God is with you,' the angel whispered. 'You have nothing to fear.' And a smile ignited on one cheek and burned like a fuse across his face. Then the angel took them by the hand and led them on a walking tour of the fiery furnace. They shuffled their feet through white, hot coals. They ran their hands along red, hot walls. They filled their lungs with black, hot air. And they blew out fat smoke rings!

Meanwhile, outside the furnace, Nebuchadnezzar's lips were no longer twisted in an angry snarl. No, they hung open and limp with amazement.

'I thought we threw three men into the furnace,' he said. 'But, look, there are four men in there now.'

The herald crept closer and looked. Then he turned to the king, his face red with the heat and dripping with sweat.

'It is an angel, your majesty. A creature from heaven. Perhaps even the god these men refused to forget. If so, he is a very powerful god indeed, for they are unharmed!'

Nebuchadnezzar leaped to his feet and ordered Shadrach, Meshach and Abednego to come out. They waded through the flames to the mouth of the furnace, kicking coals as they walked. But when they went to thank the angel, he just smiled and turned to smoke in their hands, leaving nothing but a whisper that curled around their heads, then disappeared.

'Don't forget. God is with you.'

Immediately, the officials gathered round them to have a closer look.

The satraps and the prefects inspected them carefully. 'Not a trace of smoke!' they noted.

The councillors and governors touched their hair. 'Not even singed!' they observed.

The big shots and hobnobs smelled their clothes. 'Fresh as a Babylonian spring!' they cried.

Finally, the king himself spoke up.

'Praise be to the God of Shadrach, Meshach and Abednego – the Supreme God! They did not forget him and he did not forget them – but sent his angel to save them. I therefore order that, from now on, anyone who says anything bad about this God shall be chopped up into tiny little pieces. And what is more, I shall promote Shadrach, Meshach and Abednego to even higher positions in my kingdom.

Then he looked squarely at the three friends.

'Surely,' he grinned. 'You can say yes to that?'

Shadrach looked at Meshach.
Meshach looked at Abednego.
Abednego looked at Shadrach.
Then, together, they looked at the king.

'NO... problem!' they said.

Songs in Search of a Tune:
There Was an Angel

(Daniel 3, John 5, Acts 12, Luke 24)

Telling tips: Another one to do on your own.

Verse 1:

There was an angel in the fire,
There was an angel in the fire,
There was an angel in the fire,
Walking through the flame.

There was an angel in the fire,
There was an angel in the fire,
There was an angel in the fire,
And I heard him call my name.

And I heard him call my name.
And I heard him call my name.

There was an angel in the fire,
Walking through the flame.

Verse 2:

There was an angel on the water,
There was an angel on the water,
There was an angel on the water,
And it rippled at his touch.

There was an angel on the water,
There was an angel on the water,
There was an angel on the water –
I want to feel that touch so much.

I want to feel that touch so much.
I want to feel that touch so much.

There was an angel on the water,
And it rippled at his touch.

Verse 3:

There was an angel in the prison,
There was an angel in the prison,
There was an angel in the prison,
And he opened every door.

There was an angel in the prison,
There was an angel in the prison,
There was an angel in the prison –
I'm not locked up any more.

I'm not locked up any more.
I'm not locked up any more.

There was an angel in the prison,
And he opened every door.

Verse 4:

There was an angel in the graveyard,
There was an angel in the graveyard,
There was an angel in the graveyard –
Said, 'There's nothing left to fear.'

There was an angel in the graveyard,
There was an angel in the graveyard,
There was an angel in the graveyard –
Said, 'You won't find the dead man here.'

'You won't find the dead man here.'
'You won't find the dead man here.'

There was an angel in the graveyard –
Said, 'There's nothing left to fear.'

And I heard him call my name.
And I heard him call my name.

There was an angel in the graveyard –
Said, 'You won't find the dead man here.'

King Nebuchadnezzar's Second Dream

(Daniel 4)

Telling tips: Divide your audience into three groups – one for birds, one for beasts, and one for fruit. Let them be whatever birds, beasts or fruit they want to be, and let them make corresponding sounds and actions when you reach the relevant points in the story. Yes, I know that fruit doesn't make any sounds or actions, so you might just ask them to shout out the names of their favourite fruits. Or, you could pick one silly bird, beast and fruit and let them all just do the ones you choose. The other thing you might like to do is to choose someone to play the stump and wet that person with dew (or whatever wetting device you have at hand) every time it's mentioned!

King Nebuchadnezzar had another dream.

Another bad dream.

Another troubling dream.

Another dream that kept him up all night.

So again he called together all his wise men – his magicians and enchanters, his sorcerers and astrologers. But this time, the king must have been in a slightly brighter mood, for there was none of that nasty business about chopping up people into tiny little pieces.

Unfortunately, they still could not tell King Nebuchadnezzar what his dream meant. So the king did what he probably should have done in the first place. He sent for Daniel.

'Daniel,' he said, 'the spirit of the gods works in you and reveals the deepest mysteries. Explain to me what my dream means, please.'

And then King Nebuchadnezzar told Daniel his dream.

'There was a tree. An enormous tree. A beautiful tree. Its top touched the heavens and it could be seen from every place on earth! Every kind of bird nested in its branches. Every kind of beast sheltered beneath its boughs. And every creature in the world was nourished by its abundant fruit.'

'Sounds wonderful!' said Daniel.

But King Nebuchadnezzar just shook his head and sighed – for the dream did not end there.

'A messenger appeared before me – an angel sent from heaven. And he called out in a loud voice:

'Cut down the tree,
Strip bare its branches,
Tear off its boughs,
Scatter its fruit
And send the birds and the beasts away.
But leave the stump.
Bind it with iron and bronze
And for seven long years
Let it be drenched with dew
And dwell among the animals and plants.
For the Most High God wants you to know
That he and he alone sets up kingdoms
And knocks them down again, as well.'

Daniel trembled. Daniel shook.

He knew exactly what the king's dream meant.

And he knew just as well that the king would not like it.

'Oh, that this dream was about one of your enemies,' sighed Daniel. 'But sadly, your majesty, the dream is all about you.

'You are the tree, for your greatness stretches out across the earth. And like the tree, you will be cut down and driven out into the wild for seven years to be drenched by the dew and to dwell with the wild animals. But the stump will remain, so that your kingdom may be restored to you when you recognize that ultimate power belongs to God and God alone.

'Take my advice, your majesty. Tell God that you are sorry for the wrong things you have done. Stop taking advantage of the poor and the weak. And perhaps this dream will not become your nightmare.'

Did King Nebuchadnezzar take Daniel's advice? He did not! Twelve months later, as he was walking on the roof of his palace, he looked out across Bablyon and again was filled with pride.

'All that lies before me,' he boasted, 'This city and all its glory is down to my power and my majesty!'

And immediately, the dream came true! The king was overcome with madness, and for seven long years he was left to wander with the wild animals and be drenched by the morning dew. Until at last, sad and humiliated and alone, he lifted his eyes to heaven and asked God for help. And that's when the madness left him and eventually he was returned to his throne. And that's when he prayed this prayer:

'God and God alone is great,
Worthy of praise and honour, too.
His ways are right, his ways are just,
And those who are proud, he drenches with dew!'

Songs in Search of a Tune: Daniel, Daniel

(Daniel 6)

Telling tips: In my book *Angels, Angels All Around*, I did a retelling of the story of Daniel in the lions' den which suggested that the angel kept the lions from eating Daniel by distracting them with games. This is a sort of musical version of that story. There are lots of other body parts that you might want to insert instead of the ones I have chosen. Just be careful (not, as you will see, that I have been!) about which ones you choose!

Daniel had some enemies.
They longed to see him dead.
And so they passed a brand new law
And this is what it said:

'You must not pray to any god,
Pray only to King Darius.'
But Daniel prayed. He disobeyed.
And things looked quite precarious.

They tossed him in the lions' den,
To make a lion's supper.
But God sent down an angel,
Those dinner plans to scupper.

Now you might think the angel
Simply grabbed the lion's muzzle,
But I think he found a nicer way
Of sorting out this puzzle.

Chorus:

Daniel, Daniel,
Sitting in the lions' den.
Daniel, Daniel,
It's dinner time again!

The lion said to Daniel,
'I want to eat your feet.'
The angel said to the lion,
'They don't smell very sweet!'

'Stinky, stinky, stinky, stink –
They don't smell very sweet!'

Chorus:

Daniel, Daniel,
Sitting in the lions' den.
Daniel, Daniel,
It's dinner time again!

The lion said to Daniel,
'I want to eat your arm.'
The angel said to the lion
'Don't do him any harm!'

'Oochy, ouchy, oochy, ouch –
Don't do him any harm!'

Chorus:

Daniel, Daniel,
Sitting in the lions' den.
Daniel, Daniel,
It's dinner time again!

The lion said to Daniel,
'I want to eat your nose.'
The angel said to the lion,
'The filling's kind of gross!'

'Ick, ack, ick, ack –
The filling's kind of gross!'

Chorus:

Daniel, Daniel,
Sitting in the lions' den.
Daniel, Daniel,
It's dinner time again!

The lion said to Daniel,
'I want to eat your thumb.'
The angel said to the Lion,
'Here, have some bubblegum!'

'Chew, chew, chew, chew –
Have some bubblegum!'

Chorus:

Daniel, Daniel,
Sitting in the lions' den.

Daniel, Daniel,
It's dinner time again!

The lion said to Daniel,
'I want to eat your belly.'
The angel said to the Lion,
'Why don't we watch some telly?'

'Click, click, click, click –
Why don't we watch some telly?'

Chorus:

Daniel, Daniel,
Sitting in the lions' den.
Daniel, Daniel,
It's dinner time again!

The lion said to Daniel,
'I want to eat your heart!'
The angel said to the Lion,
'Well, that'll just make you… start to have gastric disturbances
that might well result in unfortunate posterior emissions!'

'Raspberries, raspberries, raspberries, raspberries
Well that'll just make you…'
(Make 'raspberry' noises.)

Chorus:

Daniel, Daniel,
Sitting in the lions' den.
Daniel, Daniel,
It's dinner time again!

When morning came
King Darius saw that Daniel was alive.
He made his servants pull him out
And he gave him a high-five.

He then had Daniel's enemies
Tossed in the den instead.
The lion looked and licked his chops
It was time now to be fed!

Chorus:

Daniel's enemies,
Sittting in the lions' den.
Daniel's enemies,
It's dinner time. The end.

Follow Me

(Matthew 4:18–19, Matthew 9:9, John 1:43)

Telling tips: This is one to tell on your own.

As Jesus was walking beside the Sea of Galilee, he saw two brothers, Simon called Peter and his brother Andrew. They were casting a net into the lake, for they were fishermen.

'Come, follow me,' Jesus said. 'But first let me explain how this works.

'You'll have to be in church by 10.30 every Sunday morning. You can miss the odd meeting, but if you miss too many, the others may well begin to question your sincerity. They won't mention this directly, of course, but trust me, word will get around!

'Yes, I know that you may well already have something to do at that time. It's obvious that your work schedule involves some commitment in the early hours of the day, but we trust that you will find a way around that. This is, after all, the way that we have been doing it for years. It suits our schedule. It works for us. And we see no reason to change simply because the rest of society no longer sees Sunday as sacred! So leave the papers till Sunday afternoon, forget about the car boot sales, find someone else to coach the local boys' football team, and come and follow me.'

As Jesus went on from there, he saw a man named Matthew sitting at the tax collector's booth. 'Follow me,' he told him. 'But first let me explain how this works.

'You're obviously good with money, so I'm sure you'll understand. It's the roof, you see. And the walls and windows, as well. They're in constant need of repair, so there are a great many fund-raising events you will be expected to support: monthly jumble sales, cake stalls, the odd concert (We hope you like brass ensembles and children's choirs!), and of course, the Annual Christmas Fair. And with your contacts in the business world, we'll be counting on you to solicit the occasional donation – perhaps your winebibbing friends could cough up the odd bottle of plonk for our tombola? So, what do you say? We need a new treasurer for our Fabric Fund. Why not come and follow me?'

The next day, Jesus decided to leave for Galilee. Finding Philip, he said to him, 'Follow me. But first let me explain how this works.

'The world, secular culture – call it what you will – is generally quite corrupting. So we expect you to leave that culture and join ours! You'll listen to Christian music, laugh at Christian comedians, spend your holidays at Christian conferences and even do Christian aerobics to Christian worship tunes! There will be Christian books for you to read, Christian films for you to watch, Christian fashion styles to which you must adhere, and we can even arrange for you to play football with your local Christian league. Corrupted by the world? You simply won't have the time! So leave your friends behind and come and follow me.'

'Follow me.' That's the invitation, pure and simple. But an invitation to what? To follow Jesus, or to join up with some specific church culture, to come and be a part of our Christian club? What are we asking and, more importantly, what are people hearing when we echo Jesus' invitation to 'Follow me'?

Foxes and Flying Things
and Fish Food

(*Matthew 8:19–27*)

Telling tips: Divide your crowd into four groups and teach them their sounds: 'Boom-boom!', 'Zoom-zoom!', 'No room!' and 'Tomb-tomb!'. Then bring each group in at the appropriate time, remembering to quieten them down to a whisper at the end.

A teacher – a teacher of the Jewish law – came up to Jesus and said, 'I will follow you wherever you go.'

The man sounded serious. He sounded dedicated. He sounded keen. But Jesus wanted to make sure that the man knew exactly what he was getting himself into.

So he turned to him and said, 'Wherever I go? Really? Well let me tell you then. Foxes (*Boom-boom!*) have holes to hide in, and birds of the air (*Zoom-zoom!*) can always return to their nests. But I have nowhere (*No room!*) to lay down my weary head.'

Another man said to Jesus, 'I want to follow you, too. But my dad has just died and I need to go to his funeral.'

And I know this sounds harsh, but Jesus wanted the man to know just how important, how life-changing, how costly this decision was. So he turned to him and said, 'Then follow me. Follow me, now. And let the dead bury the dead.' (*Tomb-tomb!*)

It's not easy to follow. I think that's what Jesus was trying to say. Not a walk in the park. Not a piece of cake. Not a bowlful of cherries. Or any of the other 'happily-ever-after' clichés we sometimes build in to our appeals.

And to prove his point (could it be?), he boarded a boat with his followers and sailed right into a storm.

The thunder crashed. (*Boom-boom!*)

The waves rushed by. (*Zoom-zoom!*)

And his followers cried, 'Lord, save us! We're going to die. (*Tomb-tomb!*)

'There's no place (*No room!*) for fear, here,' said Jesus. 'Trust me, and you will see.'

So Jesus stood up, stood up in the boat in the middle of the storm.

And he silenced the thunder. (Whisper – *Boom-boom.*)

And he stilled the waves. (Whisper – *Zoom-zoom.*)

And nobody died. (Whisper – *Tomb-tomb.*)

For there was no place (Whisper – *No Room*) for anything but wonder and awe.

Peter Walks on Water

(Matthew 14:22–33)

Telling tips: Teach your group these sounds and actions ahead of time.
'Boo!' (Make ghost motions and sounds.)
'Phew!' (Make a relieved motion.)
'Canoe!' (Do a paddling motion.)
'You.' (Point at crowd.)
'Two!' (Put two fingers (in peace sign, please!) in the air.)
'Shoe.' (Point to your shoe.)
'Oh, poo!' (Say this sadly.)
'Woo-hoo!' (Say this joyfully.)
'True!' (Point finger in air.)

The lines are repeated three times to help the story sink (no pun intended) in. And also to give the crowd the chance to catch on to the actions.

Peter and his friends were sailing one night,
Peter and his friends were sailing one night,
Peter and his friends were sailing one night,
When they thought they spotted a ghost – Boo!
When they thought they spotted a ghost – Boo!
When they thought they spotted a ghost – Boo!

'That ghost looks like Jesus,' said Peter to his friends.
'That ghost looks like Jesus,' said Peter to his friends.

'That ghost looks like Jesus,' said Peter to his friends.
And all of his friends were relieved – Phew!
And all of his friends were relieved – Phew!
And all of his friends were relieved – Phew!

'But if it's Jesus,' said Peter, 'then he's walking on the water!'
'But if it's Jesus,' said Peter, 'then he's walking on the water!'
'But if it's Jesus,' said Peter, 'then he's walking on the water!'
'Without the aid of a canoe!
Without the aid of a canoe!
Without the aid of a canoe!'

'If you're really Jesus,' said Peter to the ghost-man,
'If you're really Jesus,' said Peter to the ghost-man,
'If you're really Jesus,' said Peter to the ghost-man,
'Then let me come walk with you.
Then let me come walk with you.
Then let me come walk with you.'

'Step out of the boat,' said Jesus to Peter.
'Step out of the boat,' said Jesus to Peter.
'Step out of the boat,' said Jesus to Peter.
'There's room out here for two!
There's room out here for two!
There's room out here for two!'

So Peter stepped out and walked to Jesus,
So Peter stepped out and walked to Jesus,
So Peter stepped out and walked to Jesus,
With nothing but sea under his shoe.
With nothing but sea under his shoe.
With nothing but sea under his shoe.

Then Peter got scared and stopped trusting Jesus.
Then Peter got scared and stopped trusting Jesus.
Then Peter got scared and stopped trusting Jesus.
And he started to sink – Oh, poo!
And he started to sink – Oh, poo!
And he started to sink – Oh, poo!

So Jesus helped Peter back into the boat.
So Jesus helped Peter back into the boat.
So Jesus helped Peter back into the boat.
And all of his friends cheered, 'Woo-hoo!'
And all of his friends cheered, 'Woo-hoo!'
And all of his friends cheered, 'Woo-hoo!'

'You're somebody special!' they said to Jesus.
'You're somebody special!' they said to Jesus.
'You're somebody special!' they said to Jesus.
'The Son of God – it's true!
The Son of God – it's true!
The Son of God – it's true!'

One Out of a Hundred

(Matthew 18:12–14)

Telling tips: This is one to tell on your own.

One out of a hundred.
A penny in a pound.
You'd hardly bother if you dropped it,
Or bend down to pick it up.

But God would.

One out of a hundred.
Statistically insignificant.
Well within the margin of error.
Hardly worth counting.

But God would.

One out of a hundred.
A face in a crowd.
A voice in a chorus.
You'd hardly notice if they were missing.

But God would.

'What do you think? If a man owns a hundred sheep, and one of them wanders away, will he not leave the ninety-nine on the hills and go to look for the one that wandered off? And if he finds it, I tell you the truth, he is happier about that one sheep than about the ninety-nine that did not wander off. In the same way your Father in heaven is not willing that any of these little ones should be lost.'

Not even one.
One out of a hundred.

The Birthday of a King

(Luke 2)

Telling tips: Give the crowd a sound to make for each key word in each section. Let them practise making the following sounds before you begin the story.

'Parade' (Make a marching band sound, or hum '76 trombones' from 'The Music Man')

'Special place' (Say 'Location! Location! Location!')

'Fireworks' (Shout 'Ka-Boom!')

'Invitations' (Say 'RSVP!')

'Presents' (Say 'For me?' or make a big unwrapping sound.)

'Party' (Shout and cheer or say 'It's Party Time!')

What do you do for the birthday of a king?

You have a parade.

With fancy floats, and marching bands and giant bouncing balloons.

Jesus was a king.

And there was a parade for his birthday, too.

A long walk from Nazareth, way down south to Bethlehem.

A caravan of people, off to pay their taxes.

Rich and poor.

Old and young.

Men and women.

And one couple in particular – a man named Joseph, and Mary, his very pregnant wife.

What do you do for the birthday of a king?
You have a parade.

What do you do for the birthday of a king?
You find a special place.
A ballroom, maybe – with marble floors and painted ceilings and gold chandeliers.
Jesus was a king.
And his parents found a special place for his birthday, too.
There were no ballrooms. And the hotel rooms were all full. But there was room in an empty stable.
With a dirt floor.
And a wooden roof.
And a dangling cobweb or two.
What do you do for the birthday of a king?
You find a special place.

What do you do for the birthday of a king?
You shoot off fireworks!
You fill the sky with pinwheels and daisies and a rumbling rocket racket.
Jesus was a king.
And there were fireworks at his birthday, too.
Shooting stars,
Heavenly hosts,
And a great big angel band!
What do you do for the birthday of a king?
You shoot off fireworks!

What do you do for the birthday of a king?
You send out invitations.
To dukes and knights and lords and ladies.
Very important guests.
Jesus was a king.

And there were invitations to his birthday, too.
'You are invited,' said the angel to the shepherds,
'To a stable in the town of Bethlehem.'
'You are invited,' said the angel to the shepherds and their sheep.
'There will be plenty of straw for all!'
What do you do for the birthday of a king?
You send out invitations.

What do you do for the birthday of a king?
You bring presents.
Bright and shiny things.
Fun and fancy things.
No boring things, like pants or socks.
Jesus was a king.
And he got presents, too.
His father's care.
His mother's love.
And a very nice set of swaddling clothes (whatever they are!).
What do you do for the birthday of a king?
You bring presents.

What do you do for the birthday of a king?
You throw a party.
You eat treats and sing songs and give gifts.
And every member of the royal family is there.
Jesus is a king.
And every year, we throw a party for him.
A party that goes right round the world!
We eat treats and sing songs and give gifts.
And every member of the royal family is there –
His brothers and sisters, you and me!
What do we do for the birthday of a king?
We throw a party.
And we call it Christmas.

Every Baby Wants

(Luke 2)

Telling tips: I came up with this just after Christmas while listening to a CD by *The Innocence Mission*. I just imagined women from all over the world, holding their babies, and Mary holding her baby, too. You could just read this one, but if you have access to the technology, I think it would be really effective to show a picture of a mum and her baby to go with each line in the first section as you read it. It would be good to use pictures of mums from a variety of different cultures. And then, in the second section, you could show pictures of Mary and the baby Jesus.

Every baby wants
To be held safe and warm,
To hear her first lullaby,
To drink from his mother's breast,
To snuggle up against a soft blanket,
To sleep and dream a dream of peace.

So maybe that is why
When God came to visit,
He came to us as a baby.

To be held safe and warm,
To hear his first lullaby,

To drink from his mother's breast,
To snuggle up against a soft blanket,
And to dream with us a dream of peace.

Midnight – A Meditation for Christmas (or Good Friday!)

(Luke 2:1–20, John 3:1–21, Luke 22)

Telling tips: This is one to tell on your own. The first time I used it, I wove it into a service and separated the three sections with songs and prayers.

Midnight One

It's midnight, and the stillness is ripped by the first wailing breath of a newborn baby. A traveller, asleep in the inn, stirs and turns over and pulls his blanket up around his shoulders. A dog sits up and barks. A child, sickly and half awake, calls for a drink of water.

It's midnight, and on a hillside outside the town only the sheepdogs have heard the cry. Their masters are stretched out around the campfire, talking and laughing and sharing a drink – keeping the night at bay, along with the wolves and bears. But they're tired and so, gradually, their talk winds down to a murmur. The hillside is still now. Still, like the town. It's midnight. And things happen at midnight.

As if to echo the baby's cry, or maybe even to answer it, the silence is torn again – but, this time, by a very different kind of voice.

'Don't be afraid,' the voice says. And if the shepherds weren't so terrified, they might just burst out laughing. Don't be afraid? Don't be ridiculous! The blanket of night has been yanked off their backs and replaced by a vision of heaven-only-knows-what! And it tells them not to be afraid.

'Listen,' the voice goes on. 'I have good news for you, and for everyone else, as well. Today is the Messiah's birthday. And Bethlehem is his birthplace!'

What can the shepherds say? What can they do? They know how to deal with thieves and bears, but night visitors like this are well beyond their expertise.

'Here is how you will know what I say is true,' the angel continues. 'Look for a cowshed. Look for a manger. And that's where you'll find the baby!'

And the shepherds are even more confused – for it's not the place that any of them would have thought of finding a baby, much less a Messiah. But then, there's not much time to think, because the next few moments are like a multiplication table of the first – more angels, more light, more sound and a song this world won't hear the likes of again until eternity.

When it's all over, the shepherds hurry off, flock and all, as fast as feet and hooves will carry them. Innkeepers are awakened and late-night revellers stopped until the shepherds finally find directions to the stable they've been looking for.

The angel was right, of course – right down to the swaddling cloth! And there he is – the baby, the sign, the Messiah!

What follows is a lot of handshaking and backslapping, and baa-ing and barking to boot. And then, not waiting around for the wise men (as some tableaux suggest!), the shepherds rush off to share their good news with the rest of the town.

They didn't understand fully what they had just experienced. And they wouldn't for another thirty years or so. But they were sure of one thing. It was midnight. And at midnight, things happen. God breaks the back of night and calls forth a brand new day.

Midnight Two

It's midnight, and there's a baby crying again. Two men, deep in thought and discussion, lift their heads and listen. One of them thinks, 'Why doesn't somebody shut that kid up?' The other one just smiles. It's midnight. And he knows – at midnight, things happen.

'Nicodemus,' he says, 'If you're ever going to see the kingdom of God, you're going to have to be born all over again. Like a newborn baby, you're going to have to start fresh – seeing God and this world and yourself in a completely new and different way.'

Nicodemus can't quite get his head round that. The baby's still crying – there's a light on now – and what began as a secret midnight rendezvous between a radical rabbi and a highly respected member of the religious establishment is in danger of being seriously compromised. Born again? Born again? What do nappies and baby wipes have to do with God?

Jesus tries again.

'The world is in darkness,' he says. 'Dark as midnight. People go their own way and do their own thing without regard for the needs of others or the will of God.'

Nicodemus has read the papers. He watched *Newsnight* before he came out. The darkness he understands.

'Thirty years ago, Nicodemus, God sent a light into this dark world, a light to chase away the darkness and lead us to a brand new day. I am that light, Nicodemus, but I've got to tell you that we have all developed such good night vision that some of us are still going to prefer the darkness. That's why I say that you must be born again. Because anything short of a brand new start – any compromise with the darkness – is a return to midnight.'

Scurrying home, darting from pillar to pillar, Nicodemus still doesn't quite understand what he has just heard. But he's sure of one thing. It's midnight. And at midnight things happen. God is up to something here. And he wants to be part of it – to leave the darkness behind and find that brand new day.

Midnight Three

'Tis midnight, and on Olive's brow,
The star is dimmed that lately shown:
'Tis midnight in the garden now,
The suff'ring saviour prays alone.

It's midnight, and at midnight things happen. Thirty-three years on, and the baby whose first breath disturbed Bethlehem's sleep is less than twenty-four hours from his last. One of his closest friends has betrayed him. There is a crowd coming to arrest him. And the followers who have sworn to defend him are asleep. There are no shepherds on the way, no guiding star above. For all practical purposes, he is alone.

What the angels sang about so joyfully all those years ago must now come to pass. He must be the Messiah, redeemer and saviour, but in a way that not even the angels could have imagined. He smiles at the irony of it. To be the Prince of Peace has little to do with living a peaceful life. There has been plenty of bother and misunderstanding and controversy – and now, finally, this.

There is a part of him that wants to run off – off into the darkness. But he is confident, because he has prayed, that nothing but his death will bring that darkness to an end.

He can see torches now, slicing through the night in his direction. He is a torch, as well, about to be consumed for his father's sake, and for the sake of the world.

As the arresting soldiers obey their orders, they have no idea what they are doing – and understand even less what God is doing. For it's midnight, and he is up to something again. He sent the baby to Bethlehem, the rabbi to the religious leader, and now he sends his own Son to a cross, that those soldiers and a world just like them might have their darkness turned to light.

Because it's midnight. And at midnight, things happen.

One day ends. And a brand new day is born.

The Parable of the Great Feast

(Luke 14:15–24)

Telling tips: We're always telling audiences to turn off their mobile phones. What's fun about this story is that you get to ask the crowd to turn them on! This will only work in a setting where people know one another reasonably well. Ask for three volunteers who have the numbers in their phone memory of three other volunteers in the room. Then get them to ring those people at the appropriate moment in the story.

If people don't know each other well, just divide the crowd into three groups and let them make 'ring tone' sounds – choose whatever tunes you like! Also tell the crowd that they need to cheer at the end, do the 'oooh-arrr' sound and make a gobbling sound, as well. Because I first did this story at the church I pastor, I used cakes and names from people in the congregation (Alan Ridout keeps bees, Joan Hunt makes a killer ginger cake, Julie Harris a brilliant apple cake and nearly everyone in the church frequents Berkeleys, our local café, which is famous for its blueberry cheesecake, and which is open Monday to Saturday from 9 to 6 and in the evenings till 11 from Wednesday to Saturday. Reservations may be required.) I think it's lots of fun to weave local details into a story. It helps to bring your audience into the story just that little bit more. So you might want to think up details like this from your own setting. Or you might just want to omit that section altogether!

Once upon a time, there lived a king who decided to host a great banquet. He sent out invitations to some very important guests. Then he commanded his servants to fetch the finest food from the four corners of his kingdom.

Honey cakes from the Rivers of Ridout.

Ginger cakes from the House of Hunt.

Apple cakes from the Hamlet of Harris.

And blueberry cheesecakes from the kitchens of Berkeley Castle.

When all was ready, he sent his servants out again to tell his guests that the time had come.

The servants came to the first guest. But as soon as they'd opened their mouths, the man's phone began to ring (*mobile phone sound*).

'I'm very sorry,' he said. 'That was my estate agent. I've just bought a field (The prices are coming down – don't you know!), and I must go and see it. Tell your master that I cannot come to his banquet.'

The servants came to the next guest. But as soon as they'd opened their mouths, her phone began to ring, too (*mobile phone sound*).

'I'm very sorry,' she said. 'That was my stockbroker. I've just bought shares in the cattle market and we need to take care of some paperwork. Tell your master that I cannot come to his banquet.'

So the servants went to the next guest. And it was just the same. As soon as they'd opened their mouths to speak, his phone rang, as well (*mobile phone sound*).

'I'm very sorry,' he said. 'That was my wife. We've just got married you see, and we need to spend some quality time together – at IKEA. Tell your master that I cannot come to his banquet.'

When the king heard all these excuses, he was furious! His banquet was ready, the hall was a picture, and the cakes looked amazing. And so he came up with another idea.

'Go into the streets and the alleys,' he said to his servants, 'and invite the poor, the blind and the lame to my feast!'

So that's what the servants did. They went into the alleys and the streets. And when the poor received their invitations, they cheered. When the blind heard the news, they cheered even louder. And when the servants spoke to the lame, they cheered loudest of all!

They followed the servants to the banquet hall, but when they had all sat down, there were still more empty seats.

'Go out to the country!' ordered the king. 'To the roads and to the lanes. And invite the country folk, as well.'

So the servants went to the country. And when the country folk received their invitations, they all said 'Oooh-arrr!'

And the poor and the blind and the lame and the country folk gobbled down the delicious cakes (*gobble sounds*). And apart from the guests who had made their excuses, they all lived happily ever after.

The Prodigal

(Luke 15:11–32)

Telling tips: Teach your group these sounds and actions ahead of time.

'Foo!' (Put hands on hips, show a disgusted look on face.)

'Two.' (Put two (as in peace sign!) fingers in the air.)

'Ooh!' (Say this in a high–pitched lady's voice, with hands on hips.)

'Blue!' (Put lower lip out, use sad voice.)

'Eeugh!' (Pinch nose with fingers.)

'Crew.' (Salute while saying 'Crew.')

'Do!' (Swing arm, with fist clenched, in a determined fashion in front of the body while saying 'Do!')

'Flew!' (Flap bent arms as wings, with fingertips stuck in armpits.)

(Option: 'Rue?' (Put finger to chin, in thinking style.)

'Phew!' (Wipe hand across forehead in a relieved manner.)

'Moo!' (Put fingers as cow horns at both sides of head.)

'Woo-hoo!' (Say joyfully.)

As in other stories of this kind, the lines get repeated three times to help the story stick and also to give the crowd a chance to catch on to and enjoy the actions.

There once was a man who had two sons.
There once was a man who had two sons.
There once was a man who had two sons.

But the younger son was fed up. *(Foo!)*
But the younger son was fed up. *(Foo!)*
But the younger son was fed up. *(Foo!)*

I want half of your money,' the younger son said.
I want half of your money,' the younger son said.
I want half of your money,' the younger son said.
So the father divided it in two. *(Two.)*
So the father divided it in two. *(Two.)*
So the father divided it in two. *(Two.)*

The son took the money and went far away.
The son took the money and went far away.
The son took the money and went far away.
And wasted it on wine and women. *(Ooh!)*
And wasted it on wine and women. *(Ooh!)*
And wasted it on wine and women. *(Ooh!)*

Then the money ran out and a famine came.
Then the money ran out and a famine came.
Then the money ran out and a famine came.
And the son turned kind of blue. *(Blue!)*
And the son turned kind of blue. *(Blue!)*
And the son turned kind of blue. *(Blue!)*

The son went to work for a local farmer.
The son went to work for a local farmer.
The son went to work for a local farmer.
And had to clear up piggy poo. *(Eeugh!)*
And had to clear up piggy poo. *(Eeugh!)*
And had to clear up piggy poo. *(Eeugh!)*

I've really messed up,' said the son to himself.
I've really messed up,' said the son to himself.

'I've really messed up,' said the son to himself.
'I'm worse off than my father's crew.' (*Crew.*)
'I'm worse off than my father's crew.' (*Crew.*)
'I'm worse off than my father's crew.' (*Crew.*)

'I'll go back and beg to be one of his servants.'
'I'll go back and beg to be one of his servants.'
'I'll go back and beg to be one of his servants.'
'That's exactly what I'll do.' (*Do!*)
'That's exactly what I'll do.' (*Do!*)
'That's exactly what I'll do.' (*Do!*)

So the son headed back to his father's house.
So the son headed back to his father's house.
So the son headed back to his father's house.
He ran, he raced, he flew! (*Flew!*)
He ran, he raced, he flew! (*Flew!*)
He ran, he raced, he flew! (*Flew!*)
(Option: Was this a decision he would rue?)

The father was waiting and saw his son coming.
The father was waiting and saw his son coming.
The father was waiting and saw his son coming.
And welcomed him with open arms. (*Phew!*)
And welcomed him with open arms. (*Phew!*)
And welcomed him with open arms. (*Phew!*)

Then the father gave him a ring and a robe.
Then the father gave him a ring and a robe.
Then the father gave him a ring and a robe.
And a roast beef dinner, too! (*Moo!*)
And a roast beef dinner, too! (*Moo!*)
And a roast beef dinner, too! (*Moo!*)

t's like you were dead,' the father said.
t's like you were dead,' the father said.
t's like you were dead,' the father said.
But you're alive again!' *(Woo-hoo!)*
But you're alive again!' *(Woo-hoo!)*
But you're alive again!' *(Woo-hoo!)*

Songs in Search of a Tune:
I Just Want to Drive

(Luke 15:11–32)

Telling tips: I think it was Nick Page who wrote a book suggesting that we needed to write songs and choruses that incorporated more modern imagery.

Thought I'd have a go.

Verse 1:

It's a struggle to admit it,
But I've taken the wrong road.
Gone to places I've regretted,
Where I never thought I'd go.
Now I'm leaving that far country,
Doing what I have to do.
And I just want to drive.
I just want to drive
Back home to you.

Verse 2:

I hate to have to say this
But I can't stand the shape I'm in.

Thought that things would turn out different,
That I was only made to win.
But I've lost – there's no way round it,
Lost the plot and road map, too.
And now I just want to drive.
I just want to drive
Back home to you.

Chorus:

And they say that you've been waiting,
Waiting since the day I went –
Pacing up and down the pavement,
Wearing holes in the cement.
So I guess that means you love me,
Love me like I never knew.
And now I just want to drive.
I just want to drive
Back home to you.

Verse 3:

It's not easy to confess this,
But I've acted like a swine.
Turned my back on those who loved me,
Thought of me, myself and mine.
But I want things to be different,
No matter what I have to do.
So I just want to drive.
I just want to drive
Back home to you.

Chorus:

And they say that you've been waiting,
Waiting since the day I went –
Pacing up and down the pavement,
Wearing holes in the cement.
So I guess that means you love me,
Love me like I never knew.
And now I just want to drive.
I just want to drive
Back home to you.

Onward Christian Soldiers

(Luke 23:33–34)

Telling tips: This is one to tell on your own. And, yes, feel free to add or delete according to your own prejudices and pet hates, because, let's face it, we're all tugging on the garment in one way or another.

> **When they came to the place called the Skull, there they crucified him, along with the criminals – one on his right, the other on his left... And they divided up his clothes by casting lots.**

Each of the soldiers had a hand on the garment. And with the other hand, they rolled the dice.

'When I win the garment,' said the first soldier, 'I will build a great church. And the church will reach out to the young, to the poor, to the vulnerable and we will tell them exactly how to live. And if they do what their shepherds say – and I mean exactly what they say – then they will be allowed to wear the garment. And if they do not, the garment will be taken from them.'

'The garment is filthy,' said the second soldier. 'But God wants only the best for his people. The nicest suits, the flashiest cars, the best jobs, the biggest houses. So I will take the garment and wash it and tailor it and cover it with jewels. And only those who have the faith to name the garment will be able to claim it.'

'The garment is so old-fashioned,' said a third. 'But I have heard from God himself. And he told me that I must lead a part of my local fellowship away from the old garment and that we must put on new clothes.'

And now there were more hands and more voices and the rattling of many more dice.

'Only socialists can wear the garment,' cried the soldiers on the left.

'He who does not work, should not eat,' countered the soldiers on the right.

'Only those who sing choruses should wear the garment,' sang one group, accompanied by a five-piece band.

'Only those who sing hymns,' sang another in four-part harmony.

'Only those who manifest the gifts!'

'Only those who believe in the rapture!'

'Only Protestants.'

'Only Catholics.'

'Only Orthodox.'

'Only those who come to my house group at half-past seven on a Tuesday night.'

'Only those who will eat my bread and drink my purple Kool-aid.'

'Only those who will allow homosexuals to become bishops.'

'Only those who will not.'

So Jesus looked down at the soldiers. The Onward Christian Soldiers. His body was torn, his clothes divided.

And he said, 'Forgive them, Father, for they do not know what they are doing.'

Water into Wine

(John 2:1–11)

Telling tips: Divide your audience into four groups. Get one group to hum the first two lines of 'Here Comes the Bride'. Get the next group to sing the first line of 'Red, Red Wine' (either the Neil Diamond or UB40 version will do). Get the third group to sing 'Yes, We Have No Chardonnay' to the tune of 'Yes, We Have No Bananas' (You'll have to mangle 'Chardonnay' to get there – emphasis on the second syllable, please). And the last group can do a Jar-Jar Binks impersonation with their line, saying 'Me-sa Jar-Jar'.

Tell each group its cue:

1) 'wedding'

2) 'wine'

3) 'servants' and

4) 'jars'

You'll want to lead them the first few times, so cues have been provided within the text below for your benefit.

Jesus, his mum, Mary, and his disciples were invited to a wedding (*'Here Comes the Bride'*) in Cana of Galilee.

Everyone was having a wonderful time. And then they ran out of wine (*'Red, Red Wine'*).

So Jesus' mum took Jesus to one side.

'They've run out of wine (*'Red, Red Wine'*)' she said. 'Is there anything you can do?'

'Mum!' said Jesus. 'Why are you getting me involved? It's not time for me to do this kind of thing yet.'

But Mary took no notice and went to speak to the servants (*'Yes, We Have No Chardonnay!'*) See that fellow standing over there?' she said. 'That's my boy! Do whatever he tells you.'

Nearby, there were six large stone jars (*'Me-sa Jar-Jar'*). They were used for ceremonial washing and held between twenty and thirty gallons of water each.

So Jesus said to the servants (*'Yes, We Have No Chardonnay'*), 'Take those jars (*'Me-sa Jar-Jar'*) and fill them up with water.

The servants (*'Yes, We Have No Chardonnay'*) did as they were told. And they filled the jars (*'Me-sa Jar-Jar'*) to the brim.

'Now draw some out,' said Jesus, 'and take it to the man in charge of the wedding (*'Here Comes the Bride'*).

So that's what they did. And when the man tasted it, the water had turned into wine (*'Red, Red Wine'*)!

Immediately, the man in charge of the wedding (*'Here Comes the Bride'*) went to the bridegroom.

'This is amazing,' he said. 'Most people serve the cheap stuff at the end of the feast, when everyone is too drunk to notice. But you have saved the best for last!'

And that is how Jesus performed his first miracle and showed his glory to his disciples.

He turned water into wine (*'Red, Red Wine'*).

At a wedding (*'Here Comes the Bride'*).

With the help of a few servants (*'Yes, We Have No Chardonnay'*).

And six huge stone jars (*'Me-sa Jar-Jar'*).

The Woman at the Well

(John 4:1–26)

Telling tips: I think it was John Ortberg who suggested that Jesus'
sympathy with 'fallen' women might have had something to do with
the suspicious nature of his own conception. This reading simply
tries to bring that out. If the language is too rough for your particular
group, feel free to soften it with other terms. It's important that you
carry on quite naturally from this into the text and that the text is
also read with a lot of feeling and understanding. At *Spring Harvest,*
we asked one person to do the first part and another to read the
Bible text. It also works well with just one person doing both
readings.

In Samaria, Jesus came to a town called Sychar. Jacob's well was
there, and Jesus, tired out by his journey, sat down by the well.

It was about noon. And a Samaritan woman came to draw water.
A Samaritan woman with a reputation. A Samaritan woman with
five ex-husbands and one current live-in. A Samaritan woman who
had to come looking for water in the hottest part of the day so she
could be sure she was on her own.

Jesus looked into her eyes, and suddenly, he could see it all:

The gossiping neighbours.

The hostile stares.

The eyes at the windows.

And the whispering chorus of voices in the market.

'Slut! Slapper! Slag! Who does she think she is, parading herself round here?'

'Oh, I've heard some stories in my time, but this one takes the biscuit!'

'We know what she's been up to. We know what's been going on. She can't fool us.'

'It could be anybody's husband next.'

'Go on, get out of here! Get out, d'ya hear? And take that little bastard with you.'

'You heard us, Mary!
You heard us, Mary!
You heard us, Mary!
Get out!'

Jesus looked into her eyes, and he remembered it all. So he turned to the woman, and as tenderly as he knew how, he spoke.

Read John 4:7b–26.

Another Woman at the Well

(John 4:1–30)

**Telling tips: Teach your crowd the chorus. Snapping fingers or some
light cymbals in the background during the verses is also nice!**

Well, well, well

Chorus:

Well, well, well.
Well, well, well.
Well, well, well.
Jesus met a woman at a well.

Jesus had to travel up north to Galilee;
Had to travel over hill and over dell.
He stopped for a rest in a place called Samaria
And there he met a woman at a well.

'I'm tired,' said Jesus. 'Could you give me a drink?
I've got a thirst that I really need to quell.'
'But your people and my people don't get along.
We shouldn't speak,' said the woman at the well.

Chorus:

Well, well, well.
Well, well, well.
Well, well, well.
Jesus met a woman at a well.

'If you knew who I was,' said Jesus with a grin,
'If you could even begin to tell,
You'd ask ME for water, for living water.'
'I'm confused,' said the woman at the well.

'Your water,' said Jesus, 'will quench my thirst.
Yet I'll be thirsty in an hour, as well.
But the water I give will quench your thirst for ever.'
'Gimme some!' said the woman at the well.

Chorus:

Well, well, well.
Well, well, well.
Well, well, well.
Jesus met a woman at a well.

'Go call your husband,' said Jesus to the woman.
Said the woman, 'I've no husband to tell.'
'That's right,' said Jesus. 'You've had five husbands
And you're living with a man, now, as well.'

The woman changed the subject. 'I believe that you're a prophet –
It's a fact that anyone could see or smell.
So tell me, should we worship at a temple or a mountain?
Tell me please,' said the woman at the well.

Chorus:

Well, well, well...

'A mountain or a temple, it doesn't really matter.
The time is coming when neither will excel.
But worship in truth and worship in spirit.
That's the Father's wish, O woman at the well.'

'The Messiah will set us all straight when he comes,'
Said the woman. 'Everything will be swell!'
'I'll let you in on a secret, you're looking at him, Sister!'
Said Jesus to the woman at the well.

Chorus:

Well, well, well...

So the woman went to town and announced to all her neighbours,
Her voice ringing clear as a bell.
'I just met the Messiah, he told me all I ever did.
And he was only sitting by the well!
And he was only sitting by the well!
And he was only sitting by the well!'

Chorus:

Well, well, well...

A Word About Worship

(John 4:21–24)

Telling tips: One to tell on your own.

He hardly said a word about worship.
But we talk about it all the time.
'Oh, so you're not doing that song, yet?' (said in a faux
compassionate, slightly condescending, mildly amused tone)
Or how about this one?
'So you're still using an overhead projector, are you?'

He hardly said a word about worship.
But we can't let it rest.
'Is your church "moving on"?'
'Is your worship Spirit led?'
'Are you doing things decently and in order?'
'Are you going deeper with the Lord?'

He hardly said a word about worship.
But we use it as a measuring rod. A whipping post.
Wesley, Sankey, Kendrick, Redman.
We do them all a disservice when we use them as the means by
which we judge each other.

He hardly said a word about worship.
So does he care, does he really care if we're

Chanting with the Gregorians,
Harmonizing with the Victorians,
Or chuckling with the Canadians?

He hardly said a word about worship.
So how do we know which of the following statements are true?
Real worship is when the bell rings and the bread and wine become flesh and blood.
Real worship is when the guitar strikes 'that' chord and the hands go up in the air.
Real worship is when we reach the third verse of 'Just as I Am' and the crowds stream down to the altar.
Real worship is when we're singing in tongues.
Real worship is when the pastor raises his voice and wipes his forehead with his hankie and the congregation shouts 'amen' and 'hallelujah'.
Real worship is when we pray the 'Our Father'.
Real worship is when we sit and just wait for the Spirit to move.
Real worship is when we reach that point in the creed where it says ' … world without end'.

He hardly said a word about worship.
Except for this.

'A time is coming when you will worship the Father neither on a mountain in Samaria nor in Jerusalem. A time is coming and has now come when the true worshippers will worship the Father in spirit and truth, for they are the kind of worshippers the Father seeks.'

Samaria or Jerusalem?
Prayer meetings or high mass?
Mountains or temples?
Choruses or hymns?

Like the Jews and the Samaritans, we're still stuck on style.
When all he cares about is substance.
He hardly said a word about worship.
'A time is coming,' he said, 'and has now come.'
But I've had a good look around, and much as I hate to disagree,
I don't think the time has come yet.

(Alternative ending)

He hardly said a word about worship.
So maybe the time has come
To keep quiet about our differences
And be content with what he said.

I Am the Bread

(John 6:1–15, 25–29; Luke 24:13–35)

**Telling tips: You might like to get the crowd moaning and groaning
and grumbling and mumbling at the appropriate places.**

Verse 1:

There was no bread on the mountain.
On the mountain there was no bread.
Only groaning bellies,
And grumbling tummies,
And one little lad who was willing
To share his Harry Ramsden's 'Happy Meal'.

So Jesus took the bread rolls.
And Jesus took the fish.

'Here is the bread!' he said.
He said, 'Here is the bread.'
And he spoke a prayer and broke it.
And every belly was full.

Verse 2:

There was no bread at the seaside.
At the seaside there was no bread.

Only moaning crowds,
And mumbling Pharisees,
Who wanted to see
An all-singing, all-dancing miracle show.

'Our fathers ate bread in the desert!' they cried.
'What kind of sign will shine from you?'

So Jesus looked at the crowd.
Then Jesus shook the crowd.

Verse 3:

'I am the bread!' he said.
He said, 'I am the bread.
And if you swallow me and follow me,
Then you will live for ever!'

There was no bread on the road to Emmaus.
On the road, there was no bread.
Just a long sad walk
And a stranger who talked
As if he knew nothing of the death of their friend.

So when Cleopas and his mate
Arrived at last at their home
They urged the stranger to stop and have some tea.

The stranger broke the bread
And he spoke a prayer, as well.

'Thanks for the bread,' the stranger said.
The stranger said, 'Thanks for the bread.'
Their eyes were opened.

They knew who he was!
And like a ghost or a phantom
Or an English summer sun,
He disappeared at once from their sight.

Verse 4:

So here we are – traipsing up life's mountain.
Here we are – simply sailing life's sea.
Here we are – in the middle of life's journey,
A long, long way from home.

Walking and talking,
Groaning and moaning,
Grumbling and mumbling,
And fumbling together for... what?

A bit of sunshine?
A Harry Ramsden's 'Happy Meal'?
An all-singing, all-dancing miracle show?
Or a life that's worth living,
Maybe worth living for ever?

'I am the bread,' says Jesus.
He says, 'I am the bread.
Walk with me. Talk with me.
Swallow Me. Follow me.
Come and taste and live.'

A Walk on the Water

(John 6:16–21)

Telling tips: Teach your group these sounds and actions before you do the story.

'Splash!' (Throw hands up in air, palms out, to represent water splashing up.)

'Alas!' (Put the back of your hand to your forehead.)

'Crash!' (Make a big and noisy crashing sound.)

'Dash!' (Run on the spot.)

'Mash!' (Make a potato mashing motion.)

'Rash.' (Rub arms like you've got an itchy rash.)

'Flash!' (Make a speedy motion with head and body, as if something just flashed past.)

Do each line three times, so that the story is reinforced and also so that the people have time to catch onto the actions and have more fun with them.

Jesus' disciples got into a boat.
Jesus' disciples got into a boat.
Jesus' disciples got into a boat.
And set off across the lake. *(Splash!)*
And set off across the lake. *(Splash!)*
And set off across the lake. *(Splash!)*

It turned dark, but Jesus wasn't with them.
It turned dark, but Jesus wasn't with them.

It turned dark, but Jesus wasn't with them.
He missed the boat. *(Alas!)*
He missed the boat. *(Alas!)*
He missed the boat. *(Alas!)*

Then the high winds started to blow.
Then the high winds started to blow.
Then the high winds started to blow.
And the waves fell down with a crash. *(Crash!)*
And the waves fell down with a crash. *(Crash!)*
And the waves fell down with a crash. *(Crash!)*

So they started to row – to get through the storm.
So they started to row – to get through the storm.
So they started to row – to get through the storm.
It was a three-and-a-half-mile dash! *(Dash!)*
It was a three-and-a-half-mile dash! *(Dash!)*
It was a three-and-a-half-mile dash! *(Dash!)*

That's when they saw Jesus – walking on the water!
That's when they saw Jesus – walking on the water!
That's when they saw Jesus – walking on the water!
And their legs turned soft like mash. *(Mash!)*
And their legs turned soft like mash. *(Mash!)*
And their legs turned soft like mash. *(Mash!)*

'Don't be afraid,' said Jesus. 'It's me!'
'Don't be afraid,' said Jesus. 'It's me!'
'Don't be afraid,' said Jesus. 'It's me!'
'Please don't do anything rash.' *(Rash.)*
'Please don't do anything rash.' *(Rash.)*
'Please don't do anything rash.' *(Rash.)*

So they welcomed Jesus into the boat.
So they welcomed Jesus into the boat.
So they welcomed Jesus into the boat.
And they reached the farther shore in a flash. *(Flash!)*
And they reached the farther shore in a flash. *(Flash!)*
And they reached the farther shore in a flash. *(Flash!*

Scribbling in the Sand

(John 8:1–11)

Telling tips: It might be nice to do this reading with a few other people. Someone could stand in for the man, who then slips away at the appropriate moment. A few others could be the religious leaders, who also leave. And then someone could be the woman. At *Spring Harvest,* we had a simple red ribbon slung round her shoulder that the reader gently removed at the word 'forgiven'. The participants would all need to be chosen beforehand, I think, and given the time for a little practice, to make the performance most effective. Otherwise, it would also work well if you just told it on your own.

At dawn Jesus appeared again in the temple courts, where all the people gathered around him, and he sat down to teach them. The teachers of the law and the Pharisees brought in a woman caught in adultery. They made her stand before the group and said to Jesus:

'Teacher, this woman was caught in the act of adultery. In the Law Moses commanded us to stone such women. Now what do you say?' They were using this question as a trap, in order to have a basis for accusing him. But Jesus bent down and started to write on the ground with his finger.

'Forsaken.' That's what he wrote. And much more besides. 'Forsaken. Abandoned. Just a plaything, if you're honest. You told her that you loved her, that you would leave your wife for her, that no one in this world meant more than her. But when push came to shove, when your unfaithfulness was exposed, you ran away and left her to her fate. If you were the man you said you were, the man she thought you were, you would be here now, beside her. But you weren't and you aren't. Because she was just a bit of rough, and this is just a lucky escape.'

At the sight of these words, a man, hiding behind a pillar, slipped away from the crowd and out of the temple courts. But the teachers of the law and the Pharisees refused to let up.

When they kept on questioning him, Jesus straightened up and said to them, 'If any one of you is without sin, let him be the first to throw a stone at her.' Again he stooped down and wrote on the ground.

And what he wrote was 'Forgotten.' 'Forgotten' and so much more. 'You're old, now, I know – respectable religious leaders. But have you forgotten? Forgotten your past? One of you was a stallion, once – spreading yourself all over town. One of you has a mistress, still. One of you is wealthy only because of a shady deal that ruined the business of another one of you! One of you knows and is seeking revenge. One of you spends far too much time with little boys. One of you…'

At this, those who heard began to go away one at a time, the older ones first, until only Jesus was left, with the woman still standing there. Jesus straightened up and asked her, 'Woman, where are they? Has no one condemned you?'

'No one, sir.' She said.

'Then neither do I condemn you,' Jesus declared. 'Go now and leave your life of sin.'

So the woman went. But before she did, she looked again at the ground. And now, somehow, there was only one word. One word and nothing more.

Not 'Forsaken'.

Not 'Forgotten'.

Just 'Forgiven'.

I Am the Good Shepherd – Three Sheep Stories

(John 10:1–21)

Telling tips: This one is pretty simple. The group simply needs to repeat what you say at the end of the 'And all of the people said…' lines.

The Sheep Thief

'I've got something to say about sheep,' said Jesus.
And all of the people said, *'Baaa!'*

'Let's start with the sheep thief,' said Jesus. 'That rotten, no-good rustler!'
And all of the people said, *'Boo!'*

'How does the sheep thief get into the pen?' asked Jesus. 'Not through the gate, that's for sure. He creeps over the wall, in the dead of night, when nobody else is looking.'
And all of the people said, *'Sneaky!'*

'And what is he there for?' asked Jesus. 'I'll tell you – he's up to no good. He has knives and shears and lashings of mint sauce. He comes to steal and to kill and to destroy.'
And all of the people said, *'Nasty!'*

'But the shepherd,' said Jesus, 'the shepherd is different!'
And all of the people said, *'How?'*

'He comes through the gate,' said Jesus. 'The right way. The proper way. The honest way. And he comes not to kill, but to lead the sheep to pastures green and gently flowing waters.'
And all of the people said, *'Nice!'*

'I am the Gate of the sheep pen,' said Jesus.
And all of the people said, *'Huh?'*

'I am the Gate!' said Jesus. 'I'll protect you from anything and anyone that sneaks in to steal your joy. And if you go through me, you'll find life and find it to the full.'

The Stranger

'Now let's talk about strangers,' said Jesus.
And the people said, *'You should never talk to strangers!'*

'Exactly!' said Jesus. 'And every sheep knows that. If a stranger calls, the sheep will not follow, because they do not recognize his voice.'
And the people said, *'That's smart!'*

'But the shepherd,' said Jesus, 'the shepherd is different.'
And all of the people said, *'How?'*

'The sheep recognize his voice,' said Jesus. 'And they follow him wherever he goes. And he knows them, too. Knows each of them by name!'
And the people said, *'That's lovely!'*

'I am the Good Shepherd,' said Jesus. 'And I know my sheep, too.

There are some of you here, and others I have yet to meet. And I know you all by name.'

The Hired Hand

'And finally,' said Jesus, 'let's talk about the hired hand.'
And all of the people said, *'Show me the money!'*

'That's it!' said Jesus. 'The hired hand is in it only for what he can get. It's not the sheep that are important to him – it's the pay cheque and what he can buy with it.'
And the people said, *'Bling-bling.'*

'So when the wolf comes,' said Jesus, 'what does he do? He runs away, to save his own skin.'
And the people said, *'It's more than his job's worth!'*

'But the shepherd,' said Jesus, 'the shepherd is different.'
And all of the people said, *'How?'*

'The sheep belong to the shepherd,' said Jesus. 'Each and every one of them is special to him. So when the wolf comes, he faces it and fights it off. He risks life and limb. And if he has to, he lays down his life for his sheep.'
And all of the people said, *'Wow!'*

'I am the Good Shepherd,' said Jesus. 'And I lay down my life for you.'

I Am the Life

(*John 11:1–44*)

Telling tips: This is one to tell on your own.

There was no life left in Jesus' friend Lazarus.
In Lazarus, there was no life.
He was laid in a grave,
And his sisters gave
Their hearts over to sorrow and grief.

There was no hope left in Jesus' friend Martha.
Within Martha, no hope of life left.
Poor Lazarus was dead,
But Jesus said,
'Your brother will rise again.'

There was still no hope left in Jesus' friend Martha.
Within Martha, no hope of life left.
'I believe what you say.
I'll see him, one day.
But there's nothing to comfort me now.'

'I am the resurrection,' said Jesus.
Said Jesus, 'I am the life.'
Believe what I say.

126

Live your life in my way.
And even death will cause you no harm!'

There was no hope left in Jesus' friend, Mary
In Mary, no hope of life left.
'If you'd come,' Mary cried,
'He would never have died!'
Jesus' eyes filled up with tears.

So Martha took Jesus to Lazarus' tomb,
To the tomb with her sister Mary.
'He made the blind see,'
The crowd said thoughtlessly,
'So why did he not help his friends?'

'Open the tomb,' said Jesus to Martha.
Said Jesus, 'Open the tomb.'
'But Lord,' Martha said,
'Four days he's been dead.
He'll give off an awful smell!'

'I am the resurrection,' said Jesus.
Said Jesus, 'I am the life.
Believe what I say
And you'll see here, today,
The power and the glory of God.'

'Come out of your tomb!' cried Jesus to Lazarus.
'Did you hear me? Poor Lazarus, come out!'
Then wrapped in a shroud –
The crowd gasping out loud –
Poor Lazarus walked out of his grave!

There was lots of life left in Jesus' friend Lazarus.
And hope for his sisters, too.
'Unwrap his grave clothes,'
Jesus said, 'Let him go!
This dead man is ready to live!'

What a Meal!

(Matthew 26:6–13)

Telling tips: Give the crowd sounds to make at the start of each
section.
'What a meal!' (Say 'Yummy!' or make gobbling sounds –
or a belch!)
'What a shock!' (Say 'Yikes!' or scream.)
'What a smell!' (It's a nice smell, so say 'Mmm' or 'Lovely!')
'What a waste!' (Say 'D'oh!' in Homer Simpson style or a
disappointed 'Oh!')
'What a gift!' (Say 'Thank you' or 'Cheers!')
'What a promise!' (Shout 'Wow!')

What a meal!

Jesus was eating dinner at the home of a man named Simon. His
friends were eating there, too.

What a shock!

Suddenly a woman burst into the room. There were tears in her
eyes as she headed straight for Jesus. She might have been someone
he'd healed. She might have been someone he'd forgiven. Nobody
knows for sure. But whatever the reason, she broke open a little
bottle of perfume and let it spill over Jesus' head.

What a smell!

The room was filled with it. And everyone around that table

knew that this was expensive perfume. Very expensive, indeed!

'What a waste!' cried Jesus' friends. And his friend Judas, who kept track of all their money, cried loudest of all.

'We could have sold that perfume,' said Jesus' friends, 'and given the money to the poor.' Or kept it for ourselves, thought Judas. But Jesus would have none of it.

'What a gift!' said Jesus. 'What a gift this woman has given. To care for the poor is important – yes. There will always be opportunities for that. But this woman can see that there's not much time left to do something special for me. And because of that – I promise you – her act of generosity will never be forgotten.'

What a promise!

Songs in Search of a Tune:
God with a Towel

(John 13:1–17)

You are the King of Glory,
You are the Holy One,
You are the promised Messiah,
Jesus the Saviour, God's only Son.
So why did you leave your home in heaven
Where angels and archangels kneel and bow
To wipe clean this dirty mess of a world?
You are the God with a towel!
You are the Lion of Judah,
You are the Bright Morning Star,
You are the First and the Last,
The Living One forever more.
So why are your hands dipped in dirty water?
Why are you kneeling before me now?
Why are you washing the feet of this sinner?
You are the God with a towel!

You are the King of Glory,
You are the Holy One,
You are the promised Messiah,
Jesus the Saviour, God's only Son.

So why does your side drip with blood and water?
Why are you dying before me now?
Wash me and make me clean all over –
You are the God with a towel!

I Am the Way

(John 14)

Telling tips: Another one to tell on your own.

'I'm going to my Father,' said Jesus to his friends.
Said Jesus, 'I'm going away.
But there are rooms in his house,
More rooms than you can count,
And I promise to take you there, one day.'

'But how will we get there?' asked Jesus' friend Thomas.
Said Thomas, 'Show us, we pray.
Don't leave us alone.
We don't know where you're going!
So how can we know the way?'

'I am the Way,' said Jesus to his friends.
Said Jesus, 'I am the Way.
The Father's Life
And the Father's Truth
Is in all I do and say.'

'Then show us the Father!' said Jesus' friend Philip.
Said Philip, 'Then all will be well!'

'If you've seen me,' said Jesus,
'You've seen him, too!
We've been together for years, can't you tell?'

'I'm in the Father,' said Jesus to his friends.
Said Jesus, 'He's in me, too.
In the words I say,
In the stories I tell,
In the miracles you've seen me do.'

'You will not be orphans,' said Jesus to his friends.
Said Jesus, 'You won't be alone.
My Father will send you
Another companion
So you will not be on your own.'

'His Spirit will live within you,' said Jesus.
Said Jesus, 'Within you he'll be.
Then we'll all be one,
Father, Spirit, Son –
Together for eternity.'

I Am the Vine –
A Communion Meditation

(John 15)

Telling tips: One to tell on your own.

'I am the vine,' said Jesus to his friends.
He said, 'I am the vine.
And my Father? My Father tends the vineyard.
He strims and trims,
He grooms and prunes,
And shapes each grape-bearing branch.'

'I am the vine,' said Jesus to his friends.
He said, 'I am the vine.
And you? You are the branches.
Let me flow in you – with love, not law.
Let me grow in you – a relationship, not religion.
And we will make grapes together.'

'Here is the wine,' said Jesus to his friends.
He said, 'Here is the wine.
It pours out just like blood.
Drink of me – when you come together.
Think of me – and never forget
That love gives up its life for a friend.'

'I am the vine,' said Jesus.
'Here is the wine,' said Jesus.
'I live my life,
I give my life
For you.'

Barnabas

(Acts 9:1–31)

**Telling tips: Divide the crowd into two groups. One half can
be Saul's friends before he became a Christian. The other
half can be the Christians. Also choose someone to be Saul and
someone to be Barnabas (or you could be Barnabas just as well).
Start Saul off among his non-Christian friends, and tell them that
they are to pat him on the back and cheer him when they hear the
word 'friends' and turn away from him and boo him when they
hear 'not his friends'. You will have to help lead them in this.
When he gets rejected by them, move him to the Christian side.
They cheer and boo on cue, too, and Saul is left alone and
friendless somewhere in the middle or at the front. That's when
you send Barnabas in, who cheers him (and never boos!) and then
takes him back to the Christians.**

Saul had lots of friends *(Cheer – pat on back)* in Jerusalem.

He was clever, and well spoken, and very religious.

He didn't like Christians much, though. He thought they were
wrong to believe that Jesus was God's own special Son. So he spent
a lot of time chasing them, and arresting them and chucking them
into prison.

And that made him even more popular with his friends *(Cheer –
pat on back)*.

Then, one day, Saul went to Damascus. He was looking to arrest

137

even more Christians. But along the way, he met Jesus in a vision, and his life was changed for ever. Not to mention his name – which turned from Saul to Paul.

He became a Christian himself. He was baptized. And he went round Damascus telling people about Jesus. As you can imagine, his old friends *(Cheer – pat on back)* were not his friends *(Boo – turn away)* any more. In fact, they wanted to kill him.

So Paul went back to Jerusalem, hoping to find some new friends *(Cheer – pat on back)* among the Christians. But the Christians were still afraid of him and did not trust him – so they were not his friends *(Boo – turn away)* either.

Paul was truly alone now. And then a man called Barnabas went to see him. He was a Christian. He was very generous. His name meant 'Son of Encouragement'. And 'encouraging' is exactly what he did.

He went to Paul and said, 'I'll be your friend.' *(Cheer – pat on back)*. Then he took Paul to meet the Christians. He told them how Paul had seen Jesus on the way to Damascus and how much his life had changed. So the Christians agreed to be Paul's friends *(Cheer – pat on back)* too.

And that is how the man with no friends *(Everybody: Boo – turn away)* suddenly had more friends *(Everybody: Cheer – pat on back)* than he could count!

A New Menu

(Acts 10–11)

**Telling tips: This is one to tell on your own. You might, however,
like to use a singer, or two singers, in the background to do the song
bits.**

Peter shut his eyes. And the next thing he knew, he was sitting at a
table at *The Restaurant of the Holy Ghost*. The waiter looked vaguely
familiar – Robert Powell one minute, Jim Caviezel the next, with
just a hint of Graham Chapman. But when he picked up one of
those little white towels and draped it over his arm, Peter knew for
sure.

'We'll talk later,' the waiter winked, as he showed him the wine
list and put a bread roll on his plate.

Peter picked up a menu and breathed a relieved sigh. Every item
was kosher. This was obviously a good Jewish place. And that's
when someone started playing the piano, and Barbra Streisand
stepped up to the mike. Peter hoped that she would sing something
from *Funny Girl*, but he wasn't disappointed when she chose a tune
from another film, instead.

Memories light the corners of my mind.
Misty watercolour memories of the way we were.

The waiter returned and winked at Peter again and then plucked
the menu right out of his hands.

'There's been a change,' he explained. And then he set before Peter a simple white sheet of paper, with a new list of entrées scrawled in a hurried hand.

Scattered pictures of the smiles we left behind,
Smiles we gave to one another for the way we were.

Barbra might have been smiling, but Peter wasn't. And even though he was starving, his stomach did somersaults at the sight of his new set of choices.

'Stuffed pork chops on a bed of mustard mash.
Scallops wrapped with bacon.
Rabbit stew.
Curried camel.
Breast of horned owl with a raspberry coulis.'

'Excuse me,' said Peter, waving his hand in the direction of the waiter. 'There's nothing on this menu I can eat.'

'Nonsense,' smiled the waiter. 'I can assure you that everything there has been prepared to the finest standards. Choose. Eat. I'm sure you'll like whatever you have.'

'But you don't understand,' Peter went on. 'I've only ever eaten what's kosher. Nothing unclean or impure has ever entered my mouth.'

'I understand very well,' the waiter answered. 'There's been a change. And if I say that the new menu is good, then you can trust me. Choose. Eat. And you will see.'

And now there was a different song playing in the background. A new song. Barbra was gone, and some stubbly-faced guy named Zimmerman was stabbing at a guitar and croaking out a folk song.

The line it is drawn, the curse it is cast,
The slow one now will later be fast

As the present now will later be past,
The order is rapidly fading,
And the first one now will later be last
For the times they are a-changing.

Peter opened his eyes. There were three men at his door. So he went with them to the house of a Gentile named Cornelius. And when he started to tell him about Jesus, the Holy Spirit came on the whole household, just like it had come on Peter. If God has given them the same gift as he gave us, thought Peter, then who am I to oppose him? So he baptized them there and then in the name of Jesus. And as the family went down into the water, Peter swore he could smell something – roast owl and raspberry coulis. This new menu was going to take some getting used to. And there was no question that he would have some explaining to do – to his friends back in Jerusalem. But as he hummed the new song he'd heard in his dream, Peter was certain of one thing – the waiter would be winking. He'd approve of this choice.

For the times they are a-changing.

Paul Waltzed into Athens

(Acts 17:16–34)

**Telling tips: This is a two-hander. One person should read the
Bible text (bold print) while someone else does the rest. This
story works best if the Bible readings and story parts flow
together as seamlessly as possible.**

So Paul waltzed into Athens with a tune on his lips. It was a gospel
tune – 'Jesus is the Answer' by Andraé Crouch (or was it The Jesse
Dixon Singers?). In any case, it had played well in Derbe and
Lystra and Antioch, and even in that 'prison ministry' thing he'd
stumbled into at Philippi. But would it play well here? In Athens?
The first signs were not encouraging.

**While Paul was waiting in Athens, he was greatly distressed to
see that the city was full of idols.**

So he decided to start with an audience who were at least a little
familiar with his tune.

**He reasoned in the synagogue with the Jews and the God-fearing
Greeks, as well as in the marketplace day by day with those who
happened to be there.**

And that's where he ran into a crowd who knew an entirely
different set of songs.

A group of Epicurean and Stoic philosophers began to dispute with him. Some of them asked, 'What is this babbler trying to say?' Others remarked, 'He seems to be advocating foreign gods.'

The Stoics were playing some sophisticated stuff – a bit of classical, a bit of jazz, the Blue Nile's 'Hats'. But the Epicureans – all they wanted to do was dance! Soul, funk, hip-hop, house – there was always some sort of party going on. And that wasn't all – Athens was buzzing with every other musical style. Heavy metal, alt-country, blues, punk, gangsta rap. How was Paul ever going to be heard in the midst of all this sound? As it happens, however, the Athenians were an eclectic bunch. Or maybe they were just on the lookout for the Next Big Thing.

So they took him and brought him to a meeting of the Areopagus, where they said to him, 'May we know what this new teaching is that you are presenting? You are bringing some strange ideas to our ears, and we want to know what they mean.' (All the Athenians and the foreigners who lived there spent their time doing nothing but talking about and listening to the latest ideas.)

Paul wanted to sing his song, he really did. But it occurred to him that it might be helpful for his audience to know that he understood and appreciated their stuff, too. So he took a chance and launched into a tune that had echoes of gospel, but a bit of what turned them on, as well.

'Men of Athens!' he said. 'I see that in every way you are very religious. For as I walked around and looked carefully at your objects of worship, I even found an altar with this inscription: TO AN UNKNOWN GOD.'

I have climbed the highest mountain
I have run through the fields
Only to be with you
Only to be with you
But I still haven't found what I'm looking for.

They liked the song. They really did. The Athenians were tapping their toes and nodding their heads. Some of them were even mouthing the words and doing that 'Edge' thing on their air guitars. So Paul decided to shift gears and work a little of his own tune into the mix.

'Now what you worship as something unknown I am going to proclaim to you. The God who made the world and everything in it is the Lord of heaven and earth and does not live in temples built by hands. And he is not served by human hands, as if he needed anything, because he himself gives all men life and breath and everything else. From one man he made every nation of men, that they should inhabit the whole earth; and he determined the times set for them and the exact places where they should live. God did this so that men would seek him and perhaps reach out for him and find him, though he is not far from each one of us.'

Most of the crowd was still swaying, still moving to Paul's groove. But some on the fringes were losing interest – chatting with their girlfriends, jabbering into their mobile phones. So Paul thought it might be time to switch gears again. He took a chance, a big chance for a rich boy from the posh end of Tarsus – and he broke into a rap. But he was clever, Paul was, and he lifted his lyrics from some of Athens' best – Dirty Ol' Epimenedes the Cretan and DJ Dizzy Aratus.

'"For in him we live and move and have our being." As some of your own poets have said, "We are his offspring."'

The crowd was with him again, so Paul decided to segue back into his original tune. He took a deep breath and gave it everything he had. He was Marvin Gaye looking for sexual healing. He was Aretha just looking for respect. He was Van the Man looking down at the crowd at the Rainbow Theatre and shouting out that it was simply too late to stop now!

'Therefore since we are God's offspring, we should not think that the divine being is like gold or silver or stone – an image made by man's design and skill. In the past God overlooked such ignorance, but now he commands all people everywhere to repent. For he has set a day when he will judge the world with justice by the man he has appointed. He has given proof of this to all men by raising him from the dead.'

And then, suddenly, Paul felt like a dead man, too. He was Dylan on his English tour in the summer of '66, and even though no one shouted out 'Judas' (largely because he hadn't actually yet told them who Judas was!), the feeling was much the same. The crowd turned on him. Some of them sneered, some of them booed and most of them walked out of the show. But there were a few, just a few, who came up to him after the show was over, their autograph books in their hands.

'We want to hear you again on this subject,' they said.

And there were others, who even started singing Paul's song.

A few men became followers of Paul and believed. Among them was Dionysius, a member of the Areopagus, also a woman named Damaris, and a number of others.

So Paul waltzed out of Athens, still humming his tune. And even
though they weren't quite yet Andraé Crouch or even The Jesse
Dixon Singers, he managed to leave his own little gospel choir
behind.

Paul Walked into Corinth

(Acts 18:1–17)

Telling tips: This is one to tell on your own. Cultural references will become dated, so feel free to replace the names used here with other artists of your choice.

So Paul walked into Corinth, hawking his gospel tunes, and what a shock he had! The city was a living, breathing parental advisory sticker. Marilyn Manson meets Christina Aguilera and The Notorious B.I.G. There wasn't a song he heard that wasn't shot through with violence, perversion and sex.

So Paul decided to start with what seemed like a more sympathetic audience. He hooked up with Aquila and his wife Priscilla, who'd just finished a tour of Italy. And together they formed a little trio. They made tents in the week (Every musician needs a day job!) and at the weekends they busked in the local synagogue, singing their gospel tunes to the Jews and the God-fearing Greeks. It wasn't long before Silas and Timothy joined them, as well. And now they were a five-piece, with Paul on lead vocals, of course!

It seemed like the perfect strategy, except for one thing. It wasn't what God had in mind. And it wasn't long before that became clear to Paul, as well. The Jews started booing in the middle of his sets. And when the beer bottles started to fly, Paul knew it was time to look for another venue.

'I'm singing to the Gentiles from now on!' he vowed. And he

147

marched off stage and booked a gig right next door, at the house of Titius Justus, a Greek and a worshipper of God. It wasn't long before the place was packed, and even Crispus, who'd been in charge of the synagogue and had secretly been tapping his toes to Paul's tunes, decided to sing the gospel song. There were loads of locals who joined in, as well, in a kind of Corinthian Karaoke. But their old tunes – all those Dirty Dancing numbers they'd grown up with and were cemented in their brains – were so strong that Paul wondered what it would take to make his gospel songs stick. And more than that, he wondered just how long it would be before the Jews shut him down for good.

So God came to him one night, in a dream. And the song God sang was 'You Got to Keep on Keeping On'.

'Do not be afraid; keep on speaking, do not be silent. For I am with you, and no one is going to attack and harm you, because I have many people in this city.'

It didn't take long to find out what the Jews would do. They got together and dragged Paul off to court.

'This man is persuading the people to worship God contrary to our laws,' they told the judge. And they were humming 'Jailhouse Rock', and 'Folsom Prison Blues' and 'Working on the Chain Gang'. But God kept his promise to Paul, and when the judge heard the charges, he dismissed them out of hand.

'This is a religious matter,' he said. 'What's it got to do with me?'

So while the Jews fought among themselves, Paul went back to singing his song. And the Corinthian tour lasted not a week, not a month, but a year and a half!

And the result? Well, not many people know this, but that little five-piece band became the original LCGC. That's right – the Lord's Corinthian Gospel Choir!

'I'm Different'

(Romans 1:26–27)

Telling tips – Definitely one to do on your own. It will be helpful to read the text above before doing this reading.

I'm different from you. That's all.
We worship the same God.
We read the same passage of scripture.
But we arrive at opposite conclusions.

I'm different from you. That's all.
I'm not asking you to agree with me.
I only ask that you tolerate my point of view.
But with you it seems that only assent will do.

I'm different from you. That's all.
I have tried to understand you. I really have.
But I see little evidence of that, in return.
Only stereotypes and labels and slogans.

I'm different from you. That's all.
So why do you think I'm a monster?
Why do you call my faith into question?
My ethics? My morality?

I'm different from you. That's all.
So why do you call me names?
Heaven knows, you don't like it.
And I don't do it. Never have.

I'm different from you. That's all.
So why do you judge me?
And why do you mock me?
And why do you call me
A homophobe?

Songs in Search of a Tune:
We Belong to the Day

(1 Thessalonians 4:13 – 5:11)

Verse 1:

Watching,
Ever patiently watching,
Watching for Jesus,
We look to the sky.

Waiting,
Ever faithfully waiting,
Waiting for Jesus,
To come back from on high.

Bridge:

Jesus comes to meet us in the air.
Death and sin all drowned in night's despair.
Light and love forevermore to share.
And we'll be right there.

Chorus:

We belong to the day,
We belong to the day,
Daughters so bright,
Sons of the light,
We belong to the day.

We belong to the day,
We belong to the day,
Leaving the night,
Right out of sight,
We belong to the day.

Verse 2:

Sleeping,
Our loved ones are sleeping,
It hurts when they leave us,
When we must say goodbye.

Keeping,
They're in your safe keeping,
Just waiting to greet us,
Just waiting to fly.

Bridge:

Chorus:

We belong to the day...

Songs in Search of a Tune:
Mercy

Telling tips: This is one to tell on your own.

It should have been freezing.
There should have been snow.
Thermometers should have read 13 below.
But the sun stretched its arms out
And wouldn't let go,
In the middle of March
It was 30 or so.

And that's just how you are.
And that's just like you.

She should have ignored me.
She should have said no.
I had the wrong shoes on,
She wore all the right clothes.
But the girl stretched her hand out,
She wouldn't let go.
And behind her blue eyes
Something more than blood flowed.

And that's just how you are.
And that's just like you.

And that's just how you are.
And that's just like you.
Wind blowing, wings beating,
You go where you go.
And I can't explain or deserve or demand,
I just know that grace pours from the palm of your hand
When you touch me.

I should have been happy
To recite my own lines.
I should have been left
To pay my own fines.
But you stretched your arms out,
You wouldn't let go.
It's not mercy you earn,
It's Mercy you know.

And that's just how you are.
And that's just like you.

And that's just how you are.
And that's just like you.
Wind blowing, wings beating,
You go where you go.
And I can't explain or deserve or demand,
I just know that grace pours from the palm of your hand
When you touch me.

More titles by Bob Hartman:

TELLING THE BIBLE

Praise for *Telling the Bible*:

'Bob Hartman is to storytelling what David Beckham is to football. An absolute master. Give him a story and no one will bend it like him.'
Pete Meadows, Head of Church Action, World Vision UK

'Bob Hartman's gift in the art of storytelling combines the richness of his experience with his unique skill and profoundly touches both adults and children alike. We heartily recommend this work to all who are children at heart.'
Ishmael and Irene Smale, children's ministry experts

ISBN: 0 7459 5124 4

ANYONE CAN TELL A STORY

'Four words. That's all it takes. And bodies lean forward,
heads jerk to attention, eyes focus, and off you go!...
'Once upon a time' can take you anywhere.'

Beginning a story is easy, but what next? Don't you sometimes long
for something different to catch the attention and imagination of
your listeners? If so, this book is what you've been waiting for.

'At long last a book on how to tell stories from Bob Hartman...
A very easy read, his own inimitable sense of humour helps to
make it so. For getting you up and running this has to be the
book. Experienced tellers might like it on their shelves too.'
Des Chamley, Facts & Fiction

ISBN: 0 7459 4587 2

Also available from Lion Hudson:

A POCKET GUIDE TO THE BIBLE
Kevin O'Donnell

The Bible can seem mysterious and overwhelming. Many people want to understand it better, but don't have the time to study it in depth.

This book can help. Presented in a handy, easy-to-use format, it takes the reader step by step through the Bible, helping them to understand the key subjects and types of book it contains, and provides a chart of suggested parts of the Bible to begin reading.

'This is a marvel of scholarly compression and clarity; but it's more than that, because it helps the reader understand the Bible as a theological whole... the perfect gift for someone just beginning to read the Bible seriously...'
Rowan Willams, Archbishop of Canterbury

ISBN: 0 7459 5131 7

THE BIBLE FROM SCRATCH
Simon Jenkins

For all who find the Bible a bit daunting, *The Bible from Scratch* could be just what's needed. Simon Jenkins offers a lightning sketch of the Bible using easy-to-follow graphics, and explains clearly and simply the essential meaning of every Bible book. He provides helpful hints for understanding what each biblical writer was aiming to get across to their readers and introduces all the famous people and events in the Bible story.

'Simon Jenkins has managed, quite remarkably, to sum up the whole of the Bible in a series of entertaining hand written pages, peppered with cartoons and humorous asides.'
Church of England Newspaper

ISBN: 0 7459 4154 0

All Lion Books are available from your local bookshop,
or can be ordered via our website or from Marston Book
Services. For a free catalogue, showing the complete list
of titles available, please contact:

Customer Services
Marston Book Services
PO Box 269
Abingdon
Oxon
OX14 4YN

Tel: 01235 465500
Fax: 01235 465555

Our website can be found at:
www.lionhudson.com